Language for Everyday Life

Literacy Reproducible Book

SERIES DIRECTOR
Jayme Adelson-Goldstein

Introductory Level

Kathleen Santopietro Weddel

OXFORD
UNIVERSITY PRESS

OXFORD
UNIVERSITY PRESS

198 Madison Avenue
New York, NY 10016 USA

Great Clarendon Street, Oxford OX2 6DP UK

Oxford University Press is a department of the University of Oxford.
It furthers the University's objective of excellence in research,
scholarship, and education by publishing worldwide in

Oxford New York

Auckland Cape Town Dar es Salaam Hong Kong Karachi
Kuala Lumpur Madrid Melbourne Mexico City Nairobi
New Delhi Shanghai Taipei Toronto

With offices in

Argentina Austria Brazil Chile Czech Republic France Greece
Guatemala Hungary Italy Japan Poland Portugal Singapore
South Korea Switzerland Thailand Turkey Ukraine Vietnam

Oxford and Oxford English are registered trademarks of
Oxford University Press

Editorial Director: Sally Yagan
Senior Publishing Manager: Stephanie Karras
Head of Project and Development Editors: Karen Horton
Managing Editor: Sharon Sargent
Project Editor: Brandon Lord
Design Director: Robert Carangelo
Manufacturing Manager: Shanta Persaud
Design Manager: Maj-Britt Hagsted
Project Manager: Allison Harm
Manufacturing Controller: Zai Jawat Ali
Compositor: Bill Smith Studio

Printed in Hong Kong

10 9 8 7 6 5 4 3 2 1

ISBN-13: 978 0 19 439886 2

Art Credits:

Argosy Publishing - 26, 27, 30, top 35, 36, 38, top 41, top 47, 54, 66, top
left 69, top 71, 72, top left 80, 84, top left 86, top left 92 Shawn Banner –
top right 45, top right 57, top right 81, top right 93 Niki Barolini - bottom
34, bottom 52, bottom 58, bottom 64, bottom 70, bottom 76, bottom 88,
bottom 94 John Batten - top right 39, top left 50, top left 56, top left 62,
top left 68, top left 74 Kevin Brown/Top Dog Studio - lower left 29, lower
left 35, lower left 47, lower left 59, lower left 71, lower left 77, lower left
83, lower left 89 Richard Carbajal/illustrationonline.com - top 29, bottom
40, bottom left 41, top 44, bottom 46, 48, top and bottom 53, 60, bottom
82 Bill Dickson/Contactjupiter.com - 24, 28, 42, top and bottom 65, 78,
top 89, 90 Kev Hopgood - 32, top 59, top 77, top 83, top and bottom 95
Dan Trush 17 Ron Zalme - top right 33, top right 51, top right 63, top
right 75, top right 87

Jayme, I will always celebrate your wisdom and kindness
as a valued colleague and supportive Series Director. Once
again, you have my gratitude.

Using a textbook written for adult learners, Josephina
Santopietro studied English to pass her United States
citizenship exam in 1948. This book is dedicated to
Josephina and so many other immigrants like her who
grace our classrooms with extraordinary energy
for learning.

Con amore, cara nonna mia.

Kathleen Santopietro Weddel

When I heard Kathy Santopietro Weddel had agreed
to author this book I danced around my office! I am
beyond grateful for her expertise, her insights and her
very hard work. Thanks also go to Sharon Sargent, Donna
Townsend, Meg Araneo, and Brandon Lord for their
expert facilitation and ability to work at the speed
of light.

I dedicate this book to Shirley Brod.

Jayme Adelson-Goldstein

CONTENTS

Introduction to the *Step Forward Literacy Reproducible Book*

Adult learners at the literacy level of instruction benefit from lessons that teach sounds and sight words linked to meaning.[1] Using the analytical approach, the *Step Forward Literacy Reproducible Book* teaches sounds and letters (phonemes and graphemes) within the content of the word, rather than in isolation. For example, the sound of *l* is taught as the beginning sound of *lamp*.

In order to emphasize meaning, the sequence of instruction is based on the language introduced in the *Step Forward Introductory Level Student Book*. This language becomes the "experience" or context which learners bring to each literacy lesson. In this manner the learners' prior knowledge is used as a basis for teaching reading skills surrounding consonant sounds, sight words, and word patterns (vowel sounds).

In Unit 1, for example, the scope and sequence of reading skill instruction is informed by the context of introductions and the vocabulary pertaining to *introductions* and *classroom directions*. The table below outlines the target sounds and sight words for each unit and the sequence of presentation related to the *Student Book*.

Student Book Unit	Phonemes Consonant Sounds		Sight Words	Word Pattern Vowel Sound	
1 Nice to Meet You	/c/ count	/s/ say	I, is, name, my	-an	man
2 How are you feeling?	/t/ tired	/th/ thirsty	are, I'm, fine, sorry	-ad	sad
3 What time is it?	/m/ morning	/n/ night	time, it, open, not	-it	it
4 What day is it?	/d/ day	/w/ week	have, thanks, see, Wednesday	-ay	day
5 How much is it?	/s/ cent	/ch/ check	how, much, the, it's	-ent	cent
6 That's My Son	/b/ boy	/g/ girl	who, that, daughter, her	-old	old
7 Do we need apples?	/f/ fruit	/v/ vegetable	me, need, here, go	-ice	rice
8 Take Two Tablets	/h/ hand /s/ sick /sh/ shoe		hello, this, what, stomachache	-eet	feet
9 What size?	/y/ yellow /w/ wear /wh/ white		looking, for, size, small	-ue	blue
10 Where's the bank?	/l/ library	/p/ park	where, next, you, welcome	-ot	lot
11 This Is My Home	/k/ kit	/r/ room	there, apartment, many, two	-ug	rug
12 Yes, I can!	/j/ job	/z/ zip code	use, computer, work, evening	-ob	job

What is the *Step Forward Literacy Reproducible Book*?

- The *Step Forward Literacy Reproducible Book* is a collection of literacy activities divided into 12 units that correspond to the *Step Forward Introductory Level Student Book*.
- The *Step Forward Literacy Reproducible Book* is effective with pre-beginning or non-literate level learners who "have no or minimal reading and writing skills and may have little comprehension of how print corresponds to spoken language."
- Like the entire *Step Forward* series, the literacy activities address the wide spectrum of learners' needs with material that supports multilevel instruction.

---

[1]The framework for the *Step Forward Literacy Reproducible Book* was based on research cited by Birch (2002) suggesting that an analytical and linguistic approach to literacy curriculum (letters in context of word and series of words in patterns) can be beneficial to learners. In this text, these approaches are integrated with the Language Experience Approach to literacy in which instructional context is determined by learner experience (Taylor 1993 and Haverson 1982).

[2]Level Descriptor: Beginning ESL Literacy, National Reporting System, July 1, 2006.

How do I use the *Step Forward Reproducible Book?*

- Each *Step Forward Literacy Reproducible Book* lesson should be used after learners demonstrate comprehension of vocabulary and structures introduced in the *Step Forward Introductory Level Student Book*.

- While on-level learners complete *Student Book* activities, learners needing more literacy-level instruction can complete the *Literacy Reproducible Book* lessons individually or in small groups. *Student Book* connections are described in detail in the teaching notes for each lesson.

- The teaching notes on pages 2–8 give detailed directions on how to conduct each lesson.

- The table below illustrates the correlation between the *Student Book* and the *Literacy Reproducible Book* and describes how each lesson teaches toward CASAS Reading Basic Skills Content Standards.

Student Book Lesson	Literacy Reproducible Book Lesson Focus	CASAS Reading Content Standards
Pre-unit The First Step	**Pre-unit** Students recognize, discriminate, and write letters and numbers.	R1.1, R1.3
Lesson 1 Vocabulary	**Letter Sounds and Words** Students match words with pictures, identify initial sounds, and select key words to remember the sounds.	R1.2, R1.4
Lesson 2 Life Stories	**Life Stories** Students read a story, recreate the story, read to a classmate, and proofread their writing.	R2.3, R3.1, R3.2
Lesson 3 Grammar	**Words and Sentences** Students match sentences with pictures, copy sentences, and make sentences using word cards.	R2.3, R3.8
Lesson 4 Everyday Conversation	**Sight Words** Students identify sight words in the student book conversation, write the words and recognize them in word puzzles.	R2.2, R2.3, R6.2
Lesson 5 Real Life Reading	**Listening and Real-Life Reading** Students recognize and discriminate sounds in task-based listening activities. Students read life-skill material, identify target sounds, and create realia.	R1.4, R2.3, R6.2
Review and Expand	**Word Patterns** Students practice word patterns in previously taught and new words. Students demonstrate comprehension in dictation and generate a sentence that will help them remember patterns.	R1.4, R1.6

Note: For complete CASAS Reading Content Standards, see the Teaching Notes for each lesson (pages 2–8).

Teaching Notes for Pre-unit Activities

Focus: Students recognize, discriminate, and write letters and numbers.
CASAS Content Standards: R1.1 Identify the letters of the English alphabet; R1.3 Read from left to right, top to bottom, front to back
Grouping Strategy: Small group
Student Book Connection: Use these worksheets after Pre-unit Lesson 1, 1A–1C in the *Student Book*.

Same and Different Exercise

page 9

 A

1. To introduce the concept of *same* and *different*, use colors. Show two pieces of red paper and say *same*. Continue with other colors. Then hold up two colors that are not the same and say, *different*. Continue with other colors. Hold up sets of colors and ask students: *Same? Different?* Model the response.

2. Draw the first row of shapes on the board. Point to the V and ask: *What's the same?* Ask a volunteer to circle the shapes that are the same.

3. Have students complete the activity independently and then check their answers in pairs. Circulate and provide feedback.

B

1. Draw the first row of shapes on the board. Point to the L and ask: *What's different?* Ask a volunteer to point to the shapes that are different.

2. Model crossing out the first different shape. Ask a volunteer to cross out the other different shapes in that row.

3. Have students complete the activity independently and then check their answers in pairs. Circulate and provide feedback.

Handwriting Practice Exercises

pages 10–16, 18–19

1. Draw guided writing lines on the board. Print the target letter on the lines, showing the students the direction of the strokes.

2. Ask volunteers to write letters on the lines on the board. Circulate and monitor.

Circle Exercises

page 17, 20

1. Put an example of the exercise on the board. Ask a volunteer to come to the board and circle the answer.

2. Have students complete the exercise. Circulate and monitor.

Listen/Point/Repeat Exercises

pages 21–23

1. Write the numbers or letters on the board. Say the first item and ask a volunteer to point to it. Continue with the other items if necessary.

2. Read the items from the Teacher Listening Script (pages 96–100) and have students point to them on their worksheets.

3. Read the items again and have students repeat.

Listen and Circle Exercises

pages 21–23

1. Write the first two rows of items on the board. Read the first item from the Teacher Listening Script (pages 96–100). Demonstrate the activity by doing the first one yourself. Then have a volunteer do the next item.

2. Read the rest of the script, pausing after each repetition. Check the answers as a group, or collect and correct students' work.

Listen and Write Exercises

pages 21–23

1. Read the first item from the Teacher Listening Script (pages 96–100). Model the answer on the board. Then have a volunteer do the next item.

2. Dictate the rest of the items, pausing as needed. Have students check their answers in pairs, or collect and correct their work.

Multilevel Suggestions

Work with pre-literate students on these worksheets while the other students complete reading/writing activities from the Student Book Pre-unit and the Pre-unit Round Table Label and Role Play from *Multilevel Activity Book Introductory Level*.

Teaching Notes for Lesson 1: Letter Sounds and Words

Focus: Students match words with pictures, identify initial sounds, and select key words to remember the sounds.
CASAS Content Standards: R1.2 Recognize that letters make words and words make sentences; R1.4 Relate letters to sounds
Grouping Strategy: Small group
Total Worksheet Time: 25–35 minutes
Student Book Connection: Use this worksheet after students have completed Lesson 1 in the *Student Book*.

A *5–7 minutes*

1. Read the words from the Teacher Listening Script (pages 96–100) and ask students to point to the pictures as they listen. Monitor and review as necessary.

2. Display a transparency. Reread number 1 and write over the 1 to model the activity.

3. Read the rest of the words from the script. Have students write the number on the corresponding picture.

4. Number the pictures on the transparency and have students check their work.

B *5–7 minutes*

1. Using the transparency, say the first word and trace over the line to model the activity.

2. Ask students to draw a line from the rest of the words to the pictures.

3. After students have finished, have volunteers take turns drawing the lines on the transparency.

4. Check students' papers or go over the answers as a group.

C *5–7 minutes*

1. Read number 1 from the script and elicit the missing letter. Read number 2 and ask students to call out the answer. Write the letter on the transparency.

2. Read the rest of the words, pausing after each one for students to write the target letter on the line.

3. Check students' papers or call on volunteers to read the words aloud and write the answers on the transparency.

TIP   Before Exercise D, use pantomime and illustration to teach students the meaning of a thought bubble versus a speech bubble.

D *5–10 minutes*

1. Elicit any words students know that begin with the first target letter, including names of friends, family and places.

2. Ask students to tell you which word they want to write in the thought bubble. They should choose a familiar word so that it can serve as a key to remembering the target sound.

3. Write the words that students choose and have them copy one word on the line.

4. Have students choose and write a key word for the second target letter. Help with spelling as necessary.

TIP   Have students enter their key words into a personal dictionary in a notebook or on index cards. Encourage students to use the dictionaries throughout their studies and to include words or pictures to help them remember vocabulary and letter-sound relationships. Dictionary entries can include the word, a drawing, a definition or a student-created sentence. Refer students to *The Basic Oxford Picture Dictionary* or another picture dictionary as a resource for pictures or spelling.

Evaluation

5–10 minutes

1. Ask students to put away their worksheets. Write the number 1 on the board. Say one of the words from the lesson and elicit the first letter. Write the letter.

2. Have students number their own papers. Then say the remaining words from the lesson and have students work independently to write the first letter of each word.

3. Monitor students' work or collect their papers.

Multilevel Suggestions

While you work with the pre-level students on this worksheet, have the other students work on the Lesson 1 pages in *Workbook Introductory Level* and/or the Round Table Label from *Multilevel Activity Book Introductory Level*.

Teaching Notes for Lesson 2: Life Stories

Focus: Students read a story, write the story, read to a classmate, and proofread their writing.
CASAS Content Standards: R2.3 Interpret common high-frequency words and phrases in everyday contexts; R3.1 Interpret common punctuation and sentence-writing conventions; R3.2 Read and understand simple sentences that contain familiar vocabulary
Grouping Strategy: Small group and pairs
Total Lesson Time: 25–35 minutes
Student Book Connection: Use this worksheet after students have completed Lesson 2 1A–1D in the *Student Book*.

A *3–5 minutes*

1. Ask pre-reading questions or introduce the story to prepare students for the lesson. For example, in Unit 1, *Are you a student?* or *This story is about a student.*

2. Read the story aloud as students follow along on their worksheets.

3. Have students read the story again silently.

4. Ask three or four *yes/no* questions to check for comprehension. For example, *Is her last name Anita?* or *Is Kathy Rose a teacher?*

TIP Students can give nonverbal responses to *yes/no* questions with *yes/no* cards. (See page T–175 in the Lesson Plans or have students create their own.) If possible, use green paper for *yes* cards, and pink paper for *no* cards.

B *5–10 minutes*

1. Display a transparency of the worksheet. Read number 1 and trace over the example to model the activity.

2. Ask students to read the sentences and circle *yes* or *no*.

3. After the students have finished, have volunteers take turns reading the sentences and circling *yes* or *no* on the transparency.

4. Check students' papers or go over the answers as a group.

C *5–10 minutes*

TIP Assign pairs so that students with stronger literacy skills work with students with limited literacy skills.

1. Display the transparency as you read and trace the example in number 1.

2. Ask students to copy the *yes* sentences. Circulate and monitor their work.

3. Write the rest of the *yes* sentences on the transparency.

4. Model peer reading by reading the four *yes* sentences to a volunteer. Then ask the volunteer to read the sentences.

5. Pair students and have them read their sentences to a partner. Circulate and monitor.

D *5–7 minutes*

1. Using the transparency, circle the period in sentence number 1 and underline the targeted vocabulary or structure.

2. Ask students to re-read their story and complete the tasks.

3. Show the answers on the transparency so that students can check their work.

Evaluation

5–10 minutes

1. Ask students to put away their worksheets.

2. Create a cloze exercise using the *yes* sentences from the worksheet. For example, in Unit 1, *My first _____ _____ is Anita. My _____ _____ is Salas.*

3. Ask students to copy the sentences and blanks in their notebooks.

4. Write the missing words in a list above the sentences on the board. Model filling in the blanks by completing and reading the first sentence.

5. Ask students to complete each sentence using the words from the list.

6. Monitor students' work or collect their papers.

Multilevel Suggestions

Have pre-level students complete this worksheet while the other students do Lesson 2 2A–2B in the *Student Book*.

If pre-level students need more time to complete the worksheet, have the rest of the class do the Lesson 2 pages in *Workbook Introductory Level* and/or Find and Circle from *Multilevel Activity Book Introductory Level*.

Teaching Notes for Lesson 3: Words and Sentences

Focus: Students match sentences with pictures, copy sentences, and make sentences using word cards.
CASAS Content Standards: R2.3 Interpret common high-frequency words and phrases in everyday contexts; R3.8 Interpret basic sentence structure and grammar
Grouping Strategy: Small group
Total Lesson Time: 20–35 minutes
Student Book Connection: Use this worksheet after students have completed Lesson 3 1A–2A in the *Student Book*.

A *5–7 minutes*

1. Display a transparency of the worksheet and direct students to look at the pictures. Say the sentences and point to the pictures.

2. Ask students to look on their worksheets. Say the sentences out of order and ask students to point to the corresponding picture. Monitor and review as necessary.

3. Read number 1 and trace the circle around the correct response to model the activity.

4. Ask students to look at the pictures and circle the sentences.

5. When students have finished, show correct responses on the transparency so that they can check their own work.

B *5–7 minutes*

1. Ask students to take out their notebooks.

2. Display the transparency and read the first circled sentence. Write the sentence on the board to model the activity.

3. Ask students to copy the circled sentences on their paper.

4. Circulate and monitor.

C *5–10 minutes*

TIP For large groups, copy Exercise C on a transparency. Cut the words apart. Model moving the transparency cards around on the OHP so that students can see the process on the screen.

1. Assign partners and give a pair of scissors to each pair.

2. Using a sample worksheet, cut the word cards apart and lay them on a table.

3. Model moving the cards around to create sentences. Read a sample sentence or two.

4. Ask students to cut the words apart. When they have finished, ask them to make sentences and read the sentences to their partner.

5. Circulate and monitor.

TIP If students have difficulty coming up with sentences on their own, help them get started by dictating several sentences and having students create them with their cards.

Evaluation

5–10 minutes

1. Ask students to put away their worksheets and take out their notebooks.

2. Write two or three scrambled sentences on the board. Use words in upper case letters from Exercise C and include punctuation. Use sentences that contain the grammar focus for the unit. In Unit 1 for example, *STUDENT. IS SHE A*

3. Write a sentence under the words to model unscrambling them to make a sentence. For example, *SHE IS A STUDENT.*

4. Monitor students' work or collect their papers.

Multilevel Suggestions

Have pre-level students complete this worksheet while on- and higher-level students do Lesson 3 2B and 2C in the *Student Book*.

If pre-level students need more time to complete the worksheet, have the other students do the Lesson 3 pages in *Workbook Introductory Level*, the Sentence Maker from *Multilevel Activity Book Introductory Level* and/or the on- and higher-level exercises on the *Multilevel Grammar and Literacy Exercises CD-ROM*.

Teaching Notes for Lesson 4: Sight Words

Focus: Students identify, read, and write sight words.
CASAS Content Standards: R2.2 Read basic sight words; R2.3 Interpret high- frequency words and phrases in everyday contexts; R6.2 Scan simple text to find specific information
Grouping Strategy: Small group or pairs
Total Lesson Time: 25–35 minutes
Student Book Connection: Use this worksheet after students have completed Lesson 4 1A–1C in the *Student Book*.

A 5–7 minutes

1. Ask pre-reading questions about the picture to set the scene for the conversation. For example in Unit 1, *Is this Sal?* or *Is her name Carla?*

2. Write the conversation on the board and read it aloud. Then ask students to read the conversation silently.

3. Ask comprehension questions. For example, *What's his name?* or *What's her name?*

4. Model the conversation with a volunteer. Have students practice it with a partner.

B 5–7 minutes

1. Write the four sight words on the board. Point to and read each word.

2. Ask students to repeat the words.

3. Demonstrate the activity by reading the first word and underlining it in the conversation on the board.

4. Have students underline the words in the conversation on their worksheet.

5. Ask two volunteers to come to the board, read lines in the conversation, and then underline the sight words.

6. Circulate and monitor as students check their work.

C 3–5 minutes

1. Read number 1 and write it on the board.

2. Ask students to write the words. Circulate and monitor.

D 5–10 minutes

> **TIP**
> To introduce word puzzles, write one of the target words on the board horizontally and vertically. Read the word to show how it is the same in both views.

1. Using a transparency, demonstrate how to complete the puzzle by tracing the example.

2. Ask students to complete the puzzle.

3. Show the answers on the transparency or ask students to check their work using the answer key on pages 101–106.

Evaluation

5–10 minutes

1. Ask students to put away their worksheets. Write the four sight words on the board.

2. Open the *Student Book* to the first page of Lesson 4. Model scanning and underlining the sight words. For example, in Unit 1, run your finger over the lines, find the word *name* and underline it.

3. Have students open their *Student Books* to Lesson 4. Ask them to find and underline all examples of the sight words. Circulate and monitor progress.

4. In order for students to check their own work, write the number of times each word is used on the page. For example, in Unit 1, *name* is used 6 times.

> **TIP**
> Sight words are words learned as complete units rather than by individual letter sounds. They fall into three basic categories: survival words (*name, computer, job*), service or utility words (*the, when, its*), or irregularly spelled words (*give, have, Wednesday*).

Multilevel Suggestions

Have pre-level students complete this worksheet while the other students are practicing the Lesson 4 1D conversation in the *Student Book*.

If pre-level students need more time to complete the worksheet, have the rest of the class do the Lesson 4 pages in *Workbook Introductory Level* and/or the on- and higher- level exercises on the *Multilevel Grammar and Literacy Exercises* CD-ROM.

Teaching Notes for Lesson 5: Listening and Real-Life Reading

Focus: Students recognize and discriminate sounds then read and create real-life reading material.
CASAS Content Standards: R1.4 Relate letters to sounds; R2.3 Interpret common high frequency words and phrases in everyday contexts; R6.2 Scan simple text to find specific information
Grouping Strategy: Small group
Total Lesson Time: 25–30 minutes
Student Book Connection: Use this worksheet after students have completed Lesson 5 1A–2B in the *Student Book*.

A *4–5 minutes*

1. Introduce the target sounds using a transparency of the worksheet.

2. Read the Teacher Listening Script (pages 96–100) and point to the target letters in the charts.

B *5–10 minutes*

1. Read number 1 from the script. Demonstrate how to complete the task by tracing the check mark in the example provided. Read number 2, ask students to call out the answer, and then check the appropriate box.

2. Ask students to listen and check the correct box. Read each word twice with natural speed and intonation. Pause after each repetition.

3. When students are finished, ask them to check their work as you read the words and check correct boxes on the transparency.

C *4–5 minutes*

For Units 3, 4, 7, 10, and 11 repeat the steps for Activity B.

For Units 1, 2, 5, 6, 8, 9, and 12 follow these steps:

1. Read number 1 from the script. Demonstrate how to complete the task by tracing the circled word. Read number 2, ask students to call out the answer, and circle the correct response.

2. Read the rest of the script, saying each word twice with natural speed and intonation, and pausing between repetitions.

3. Ask students to check their work as you read and circle the correct words on the transparency.

D *5–10 minutes*

1. Introduce the real-life reading by naming the kind of life skill material. For example, in Unit 3, *This is a bus schedule for Bus 49.*

2. Ask the students to read the material silently.

3. Ask comprehension questions. For example, in Unit 3, *The bus is at Main Street. What time is it?*

4. Model the activity by finding and circling one of the target letters. Ask students to complete the activity.

5. Write the target words on the board. Ask students where they hear the sound (beginning, middle, or end). Circle the target letters. Have students check their work by scanning their worksheets for the words on the board.

Evaluation

5–10 minutes

1. Assign student pairs. Read the directions aloud.

2. Show students how to get started on the activity by modeling it on the board.

3. While students complete the activity, circulate and monitor progress.

4. Have pairs present their realia to the class.

TIP

Display or distribute real forms, schedules, signs, etc. related to the real-life reading in the unit. To practice scanning, ask students to find and circle words from the lesson on the realia.

Multilevel Suggestions

While you work with the pre-level students on this worksheet, have the other students do the Lesson 5 pages in *Workbook Introductory Level* and/or the on- and higher-level exercises on the *Multilevel Grammar and Literacy Exercises CD-ROM*.

Teaching Notes for Review and Expand: Word Patterns

Focus: Students practice word patterns, write words from dictation, and write a sentence to remember patterns.
CASAS Content Standards: R1.4 Relate letters to sounds; R1.6 Use common phonological patterns to sound out unfamiliar words
Grouping Strategy: Small group
Total Lesson Time: 20–30 minutes
Student Book Connection: Use this worksheet after students have completed Review and Expand in the *Student Book*.

TIP Before beginning instruction with word patterns, teach students the concept of rhyming. This can be done by using a piece of realia, for example, a cap. Show the cap and say *cap.* Then give three or four other words that rhyme—*lap, tap, map.* Ask students to repeat the words while pointing to the realia. Students should repeat the words as a list rather than as individual items.

A *5–10 minutes*

1. Direct students to look at the pictures. Using a transparency of the worksheet, point to each picture and read the Teacher Listening Script (pages 96–100).

2. To check comprehension, say the words out of order and ask students to point to the correct picture or ask for locations of items. For example, in Unit 1, *Where is the van?* or *Where is the can?*

3. Ask students to point to the pictures and say the words.

B *4–5 minutes*

1. Read number 1 and trace the example on the transparency. Read number 2 and ask students to call out the answer. Write the pattern for number 2.

2. Ask students to read and write the rest of the words.

3. Read and write the words on the transparency as students check their work.

4. Ask volunteers to read the list of words aloud.

C *4–5 minutes*

1. Read number 1 from the script and trace the missing letter in the example. Read number 2 and ask students to call out the answer. Write the letter on the transparency.

2. Read the rest of the words from the script twice using natural speed and intonation. Pause after each repetition.

3. Check students' papers or call on volunteers to read the words and write the answers on the transparency.

Evaluation

5–10 minutes

1. Direct students to look at the picture. Read and ask students to repeat the sentence.

2. To check comprehension, ask students to point to specific items or ask *yes/no* questions about the picture.

3. Write the words in a list on the board. Read the list. Ask students to read the words as you point to each one.

4. Ask students to call out sentences using the words. Write their sentences on the board.

5. Have students choose and write a sentence on the line in the thought bubble.

TIP In this lesson, vowels are introduced in word patterns. For the most part, the English pattern targeted is consonant-vowel-consonant (C-V-C). Rather than sounding out words by producing each vowel individually, students can learn the phonemes as part of ending clusters because the sound that a vowel represents is signaled by the pattern in which it is found. See the Appendix for a list of beginning- and intermediate-level word patterns.

Multilevel Suggestions

While you work with the pre-level students on this worksheet, have the other students work on the Review and Expand pages in *Workbook Introductory Level,* the Peer Dictation from *Multilevel Activity Book Introductory Level* and/or the on- and higher-level exercises on the *Multilevel Grammar and Literacy Exercises* CD-ROM.

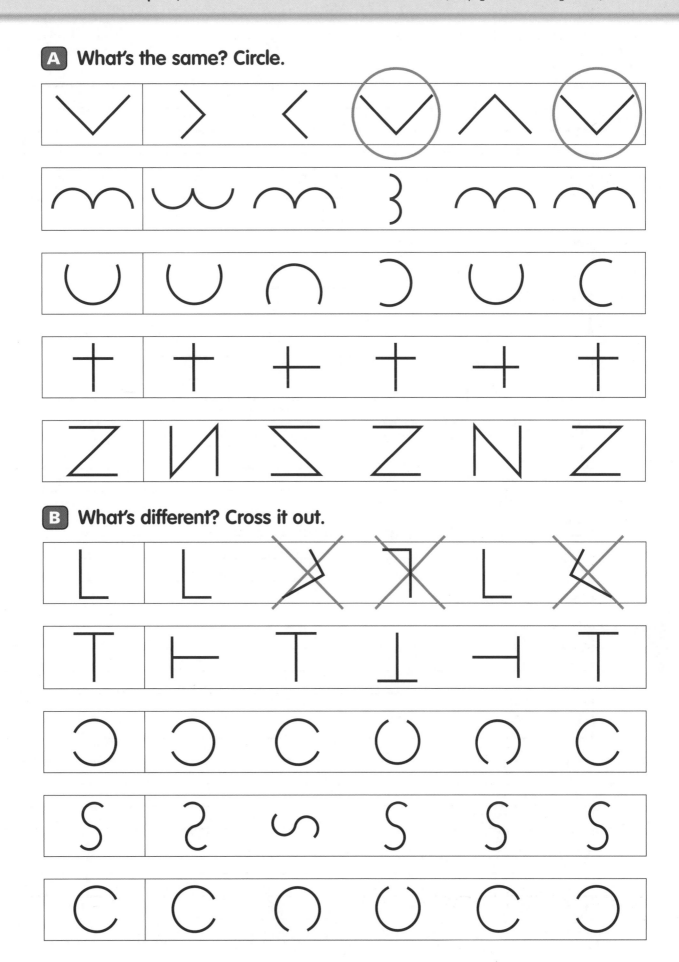

A What's the same? Circle.

B What's different? Cross it out.

Write.

Write.

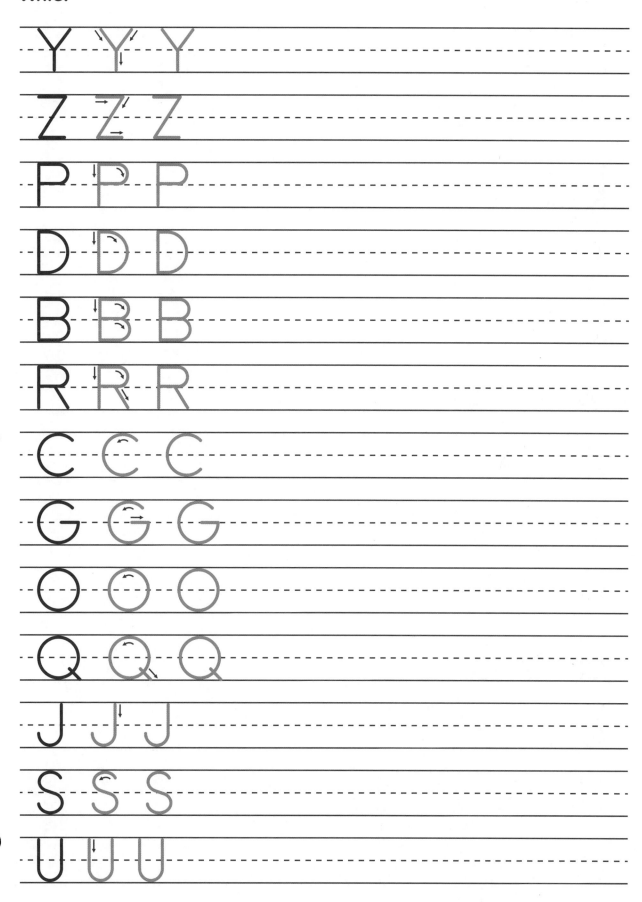

Write.

l l l

i i i

k k k

t t t

v v v

w w w

x x x

y y y

z z z

a a a

b b b

d d d

q q q

Write.

p p p

g g g

h h h

m m m

n n n

r r r

f f f

j j j

s s s

u u u

c c c

e e e

o o o

Write.

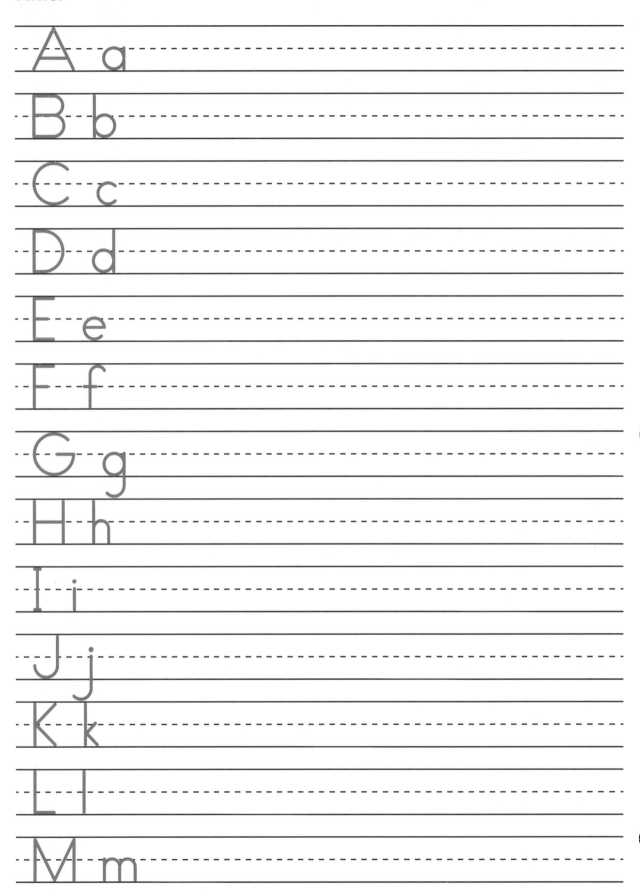

Write.

● N n

O o

P p

Q q

R r

S s

● T t

U u

V v

W w

X x

Y y

● Z z

Circle.

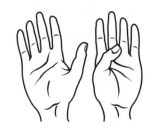

a. ⓪ 1 2 3 4   b. 6 7 8 9 10   c. 7 1 5 9 2

d. 1 3 2 5 4   e. 5 2 1 4 3

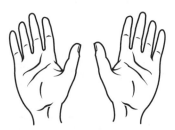

f. 6 8 10 3 5   g. 2 8 10 7 3

h. 1 9 3 2 8   i. 3 5 8 2 4

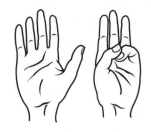

j. 6 7 5 3 10   k. 6 7 8 9 10

A **Write the numbers.**

0 1 2 3 4 5 6 7 8 9 10

B **Write the missing numbers.**

a.   0   1   2   _3_   4   5   6   7   8   9   10

b.   0   1   2   3   ___   5   6   ___   8   9   10

c.   ___   1   ___   3   4   5   ___   7   8   ___   10

d.   0   ___   2   ___   4   ___   6   7   ___   9   ___

e.   0   ___   ___   ___   ___   ___   ___   ___   ___   ___

Write.

● ONE
TWO
THREE
FOUR
FIVE
SIX
● SEVEN
EIGHT
NINE
TEN

●

Listening p. 96 **A** **Listen and point. Repeat.**

A a   B b   C c   D d

E e   F f   G g   H h

I i   J j   K k   L l

M m   N n   O o   P p

Q q   R r   S s   T t

U u   V v   W w   X x

        Y y   Z z

B **Circle the letters in your name.**

C **Write.**

My name is

_____

- -

_____

First   Last

Listening p. 96 **A** **Listen and point. Repeat.**

1. f t   4. p q   7. c z   10. j g
2. u n   5. i j   8. l r   11. i y
3. s z   6. d b   9. b v   12. d t

Listening p. 96 **B** **Listen and Circle.**

1. o e ⓐ   7. v w u
2. i j g   8. t l i
3. m n u   9. a b d
4. t f h   10. c e o
5. r c e   11. p y g
6. k y z   12. s z k

Listening p. 96 **C** **Listen and write.**

1. __s__   3. _____   5. _____   7. _____
2. _____   4. _____   6. _____   8. _____

Listening p. 96 **D** **Listen and write.**

1. ____pen____   4. _____
2. _____   5. _____
3. _____   6. _____

Listening p. 96 **A** **Listen and point. Repeat.**

1. V Y   4. N M   7. I L

2. E F   5. B R

3. O C   6. P D

Listening p. 96 **B** **Listen and Circle.**

1. C Ⓖ O   4. E O A   7. W U V

2. U I O   5. P T E   8. E A I

3. F E H   6. M N V   9. Z K N

Listening p. 96 **C** **Listen and write.**

1. _two_____

2. _____

3. _____

4. _____

5. _____

6. _____

7. _____

Listening p. 96 **A** **Listen and point. Repeat.**

a.	0	e.	4	i.	8
b.	1	f.	5	j.	9
c.	2	g.	6	k.	10
d.	3	h.	7		

Listening p. 96 **B** **Listen and Circle.**

a.	3	⑦	2		f.	10	4	1
b.	5	2	8		g.	313	303	300
c.	2	4	9		h.	205	515	552
d.	6	9	8		i.	917	719	970
e.	7	1	10		j.	198	981	189

Listening p. 96 **C** **Listen and write.**

a.   2   3   5   –   6   <u>5</u>   5   <u>2</u>

b.   4   6   ___   –   3   ___   9   ___

c.   5   ___   ___   –   4   ___   7   ___

d.   ___   ___   ___   –   6   ___   2   ___

e.   ___   ___   ___   –   ___   ___   ___   ___

f.   ___   ___   ___   –   ___   ___   ___   ___

Cc and Ss

Listening p. 96 **A** **Listen and number the pictures.**

B **Draw a line from the pictures to the words with *c* or *s*.**

clock   count   close

student   say   sign

Listening p. 96 **C** **Listen and complete the words with *c* or *s*.**

1. _c_ lock   3. ___ lose   5. ___ ay

2. ___ ount   4. ___ udent   6. ___ ign

D **Write a word to remember *c*. Write a word to remember *s*.**

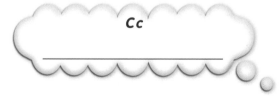

Cc _____   Ss _____

I Am a Student

A **Read the story.**

My first name is Anita.

My last name is Salas.

I am a student.

My teacher is Kathy Rose.

B **Circle *yes* or *no*.**

1. My first name is Anita.	(yes)	no
2. My first name is Salas.	yes	no
3. My last name is Salas.	yes	no
4. My last name is Anita.	yes	no
5. I am a teacher.	yes	no
6. I am a student.	yes	no
7. My teacher is Anita.	yes	no
8. My teacher is Kathy Rose.	yes	no

C **Write the *yes* sentences. Read the story to a partner.**

    My name is Anita.

_____

_____

_____

D **Circle the periods (.) in the story. Underline the names.**

Subject Pronouns

A **Look at the picture. Circle the sentence.**

$\boxed{\text{I am a teacher.}}$ I am a student.

He is a student.   She is a student.

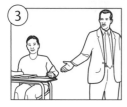

He is a student.   She is a student.

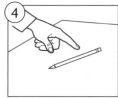

It is a pencil.   They are pencils.

He is a student.   They are students.

B **Write the circled sentences on your paper.**

C **Cut apart the cards. Make sentences.**

I AM	YOU	HE
SHE	IS	THEY
ARE	STUDENTS.	A STUDENT.

I, Is, Name, My

A **Read the conversation.**

Sal: Hi. <u>I</u> am Sal. What is your name?
Carla: My name is Carla.

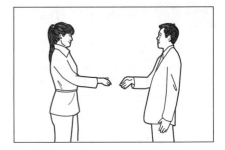

B **Underline these words in the conversation.**

I̶	is	name	my

C **Write the words.**

1. I _____I_____   3. name _____

2. is _____   4. my _____

D **Circle the sight words in the puzzle.**

B	N	A	M	Ⓘ	Y	S
X	N	A	M	E	X	N
T	T	M	D	R	M	R
C	Z	W	M	Y	O	L
M	I	B	J	P	R	P
O	S	R	D	T	F	L

Cc and *Ss*

 A **Listen for the sound of *c*. Listen for the sound of *s*.**

Cc
1. <u>C</u> L O C K
2. <u>C</u> L O S E
3. <u>C</u> O U N T

Ss
1. <u>S</u> A Y
2. <u>S</u> T U D E N T
3. <u>S</u> I G N

 B **Listen and check (✔) the sound you hear.**

	c	*s*
1.	✔	
2.		
3.		
4.		
5.		
6.		

C **Listen and circle the word you hear.**

1. close   (student)   4. say   count
2. clock   student   5. close   say
3. sign   close   6. class   say

D **Read the names. Circle *c* and *s*.**

Dr. Carr   Mrs. Benson   Sam Clark

E **Make a name tag with your name. Make a name tag for a classmate.**

Word Patterns with -*an*

A Look at the pictures. Listen and read the words.
Listening p. 97

1
can

2
man

3
Dan

4
fan

5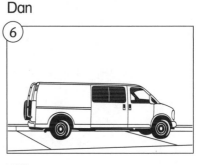
pan

6
van

B Read and complete the words.

1. can   c _an_
2. man   m ____
3. Dan   D ____

4. fan   f ____
5. pan   p ____
6. van   v ____

C Listen and complete the words.
Listening p. 97

1. _c_ an
2. ___ an

3. ___ an
4. ___ an

5. ___ an
6. ___ an

D Write a sentence to remember the –*an* sound.

The man puts the fan in the van.

Your sentence

_____

_____

Tt and *TH/th*

Listening
p. 97 **A** Listen and number the pictures.

B Draw a line from the pictures to the words with *t* or *th*.

tired   teacher   ten

thirsty   they   three

Listening
p. 97 **C** Listen and complete the words with *t* or *th*.

1. _t_ ired   3. ___ en   5. ___ ey

2. ___ eacher   4. ___ irsty   6. ___ ree

D Write a word to remember *t*. Write a word to remember *th*.

Tt

TH/th

I Am Happy in Dallas

A **Read the story.**

My name is Camille.

I am from Haiti.

Now I am in Dallas, Texas.

I am happy in Dallas.

B **Circle *yes* or *no*.**

1. My name is Camille.	(yes)	no
2. My name is Tim.	yes	no
3. I am from Texas.	yes	no
4. I am from Haiti.	yes	no
5. Now I am in Dallas, Texas.	yes	no
6. Now I am in Haiti.	yes	no
7. I am sad in Dallas.	yes	no
8. I am happy in Dallas.	yes	no

C **Write the *yes* sentences. Read the story to a partner.**

My name is Camille.

_____

_____

_____

D **Circle the periods (.) in the story. Underline the capital letters.**

Negative Statements with *Be*

A Look at the picture. Circle the sentence or sentences.

 ① She is tired.   He is tired.

 ② She is tired.   He is tired.

 ③ They are tired.   They are thirsty.

 ④ She is not sad.   He is not sad.

⑤ She is not sick.   She is not happy.
She's happy.   She's sick.

B Write the circled sentences on your paper.

C Cut apart the cards. Make sentences.

HE	SHE	THEY
IS	ARE	NOT
HAPPY.	TIRED.	YOU

Are, I'm, Fine, Sorry

A **Read the conversation.**

Tom: How <u>are</u> you feeling?
Teng: I'm fine. How are you feeling?
Tom: I'm sick.
Teng: Oh, I'm sorry.

B **Underline these words in the conversation.**

~~are~~	I'm	fine	sorry

C **Write the words.**

1. are _____are_____   3. fine _____

2. I'm _____   4. sorry _____

D **Circle the sight words in the puzzle.**

D	S	O	R	I	R	Y	A
M	S	O	R	R	Y	P	R
A	F	I	N	P	D	A	T
R	G	F	I	N	E	I	L
E	I'	A	U	Q	I'	I	B
X	I'	M	D	R	O	A	M

Tt and *TH/th*

Listening p. 97 **A** **Listen for the sound of *t*. Listen for the sound of *th*.**

Tt	Th/th
1. <u>T</u>IRED	4. <u>TH</u>IRSTY
2. <u>T</u>EACHER	5. <u>TH</u>EY
3. <u>T</u>EN	6. <u>TH</u>REE

Listening p. 97 **B** **Listen and check (✔) the sound you hear.**

	t	*th*
1.	✔	
2.		
3.		
4.		
5.		
6.		

Listening p. 97 **C** **Listen and circle the word you hear.**

1. (tired)   thirsty
2. ten   three
3. three   thirteen
4. they   ten
5. then   ten
6. ten   two

D **Read the address on the envelope. Circle *t* and *th*.**

Mr. Tam
City Adult School
1010 Third Street
Austin, TX 80321

E **Write your school address on an envelope. Write your return address on the envelope. Is there a *t* or *th* in the addresses?**

Word Patterns with -*ad*

Listening p. 97 **A** **Look at the pictures. Listen and read the words.**

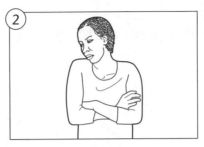
ad

sad

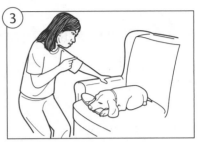
bad

dad

mad

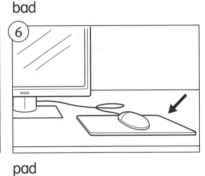
pad

B **Read and complete the words.**

1. ad   ad

2. sad   s ____

3. dad   d ____

4. mad   m ____

5. pad   p ____

6. bad   b ____

Listening p. 97 **C** **Listen and complete the words.**

1. ad

2. ___ ad

3. ___ ad

4. ___ ad

5. ___ ad

6. ___ ad

D **Write a sentence to remember the –*ad* sound.**

Dad is sad not mad.

Your sentence

_____

_____

Mm and *Nn*

Listening p. 97 **A** **Listen and number the pictures.**

B **Draw a line from the pictures to the words with *m* or *n*.**

morning   man   men   midnight

night   noon   notebook   nine

Listening p. 97 **C** **Listen and complete the words with *m* or *n*.**

1. <u>m</u> orning   4. ___ idnight   7. ___ otebook

2. ___ an   5. ___ ight   8. ___ ine

3. ___ en   6. ___ oon

D **Write a word to remember *m*. Write a word to remember *n*.**

Mm

Nn

I Go to English Class

A **Read the story.**

I go to the store at 8:00.

I go to the library at 9:30.

I go to school at 10:00.

I go to English class at 10:30.

B **Circle** *yes* **or** *no.*

1. I go to the store at 8:00.	(yes)	no
2. I go to the store at 8:30.	yes	no
3. I go to the library at 9:30.	yes	no
4. I go to the library at 9:00.	yes	no
5. I go to work at 10:00.	yes	no
6. I go to school at 10:00.	yes	no
7. I go to English class at 10:30.	yes	no
8. I go to English class at 10:00.	yes	no

C **Write the** *yes* **sentences. Read the story to a partner.**

I go to the store at 8:00.

_____

_____

_____

D **Circle the periods (.) in the story. Underline the times.**

Yes/No Questions with *Be*

A Look at the picture. Circle the question and sentence.

1

| Is she at school? | Is he at school? |
| Yes, she is. | Yes, he is. |

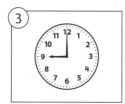

2

Is she at school?   Is he at school?
Yes, she is.   Yes, he is.

3

Is it 9:00?   Is it 9:00?
Yes, it is.   No, it isn't.

4

Are they at home?   Are they at school?
Yes, they are.   Yes, they are.

5

Is she at the store?   Is she at the store?
Yes, she is.   No, she isn't.

B Write the circled questions and sentences on your paper.

C Cut apart the cards. Make questions and sentences.

IS	AT HOME?	SHE
HE	IS.	AT SCHOOL?
NO,	ISN'T.	YES,

Time, It, Open, Not

A **Read the conversation.**

Marta: Excuse me. What <u>time</u> is it?
Min: It's 8:00.
Marta: Is the store open?
Min: No, it's not.

B **Underline these words in the conversation.**

~~time~~	it	open	not

C **Write the words.**

1. time _____time_____   3. open _____

2. it _____   4. not _____

D **Complete the sentences. Write the words in the puzzle.**

Excuse me. What _____time_____ is _____?
                        1   2

It's 8:00.

Is the store _____?
                    3

No, it's _____.
              4

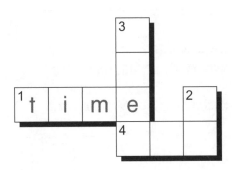

Mm and *Nn*

A Where do you hear *m*? Where do you hear *n*?

Listening p. 97

Mm	
beginning	1. Ⓜ A N
middle	2. N U Ⓜ B E R
end	3. F R O Ⓜ

Nn	
beginning	4. Ⓝ I G H T
middle	5. P E Ⓝ C I L
end	6. P E Ⓝ

B Where do you hear *m*? Listen and check (✔).

Listening p. 97

Mm	1.	2.	3.	4.	5.	6.
beginning	✔					
middle						
end						

C Where do you hear *n*? Listen and check (✔).

Listening p. 97

Nn	1.	2.	3.	4.	5.	6.
beginning	✔					
middle						
end						

D Read the schedule for Bus 49. Circle *m* and *n*.

Bus Number	Main St.	Newport St.	Mapleton Ave.
49	9:00 a.m.	9:25 a.m.	9:55 a.m.

E Make a Bus 49 schedule for three streets in your city.
Use names that begin with *M* or *N*.

Word Patterns with -*it*

Listening p. 97 **A** Look at the pictures. Listen and read the words.

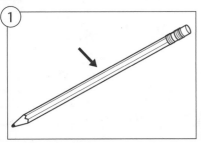

1

it

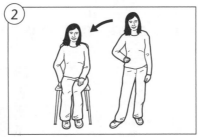

2

sit

3

mitt

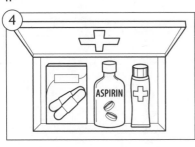

4

kit

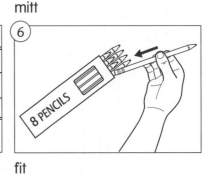

5

hit

6

fit

B Read and complete the words.

1. it   _it_

2. sit   s ____

3. mitt   m ____ t

4. kit   k ____

5. hit   h ____

6. fit   f ____

Listening p. 97 **C** Listen and complete the words.

1. _i_ t

2. ____ it

3. ____ it

4. ____ itt

5. ____ it

6. ____ it

D Write a sentence to remember the – *it* sound.

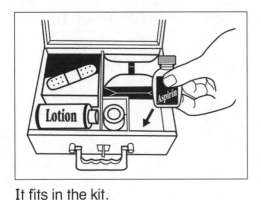

It fits in the kit.

Your sentence

_____

_____

Dd and *Ww*

Listening p. 97 **A** Listen and number the pictures.

B Draw a line from the pictures to the words with *d* or *w*.

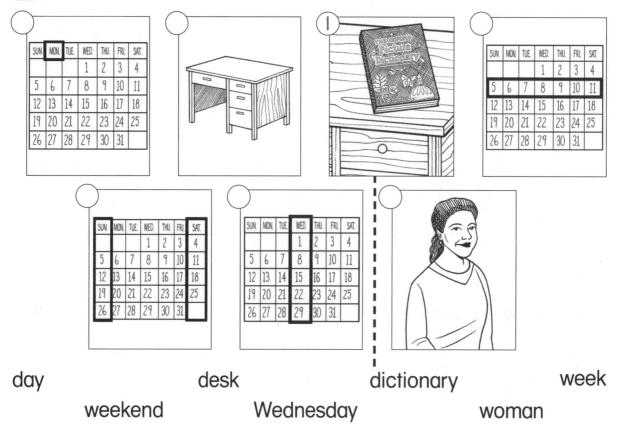

day   desk   dictionary   week

weekend   Wednesday   woman

Listening p. 97 **C** Listen and complete the words with *d* or *w*.

1. _d_ ay   4. ___ eek   7. ___ oman

2. ___ esk   5. ___ eekend

3. ___ ictionary   6. ___ ednesday

D Write a word to remember *d*. Write a word to remember *w*.

Dd

Ww

It's October

A **Read the story.**

It's October.

Next month is November.

My birthday is in November.

B **Circle *yes* or *no*.**

1. It's October.	(yes)	no
2. It's May.	yes	no
3. Next month is April.	yes	no
4. Next month is November.	yes	no
5. My birthday is in November.	yes	no
6. My birthday is in April.	yes	no

C **Write the *yes* sentences. Read the story to a partner.**

It's October.

_____

_____

D **Circle the periods (.) in the story. Underline the capital letters.**

Information Questions

A **Look at the picture. Circle the question or sentence.**

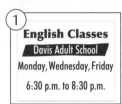

Where is the English class?   What time is the English class?

Where is the English class?   When is the English class?

What time is the English class?   Where is the English class?

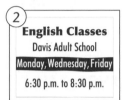

The English class is at school.   The English class is at 6:30 p.m.

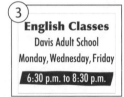

The English class is at Davis School.   The English class is on Wednesday.

B **Write the circled questions and sentences on your paper.**

C **Cut apart the cards. Make questions or sentences.**

WHERE	WHEN	WHAT TIME
IS	ON WEDNESDAY.	THE ENGLISH CLASS?
IT'S	AT SCHOOL.	AT 6:30.

Have, Thanks, See, Wednesday

A **Read the conversation.**

Dara: Goodbye. <u>Have</u> a nice weekend.

Diana: Thanks. You, too.
           See you Wednesday.

B **Underline these words in the conversation.**

~~Have~~	Thanks	See	Wednesday

C **Write the words.**

1. Have ____Have____   3. See _____

2. Thanks _____   4. Wednesday _____

D **Complete the sentences. Write the words in the puzzle.**

Goodbye. ____Have____ a nice weekend.
              1

_____. You, too.
     2

_____ you _____ .
     3   4

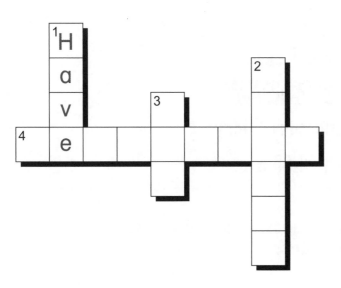

Dd and *Ww*

Listening p. 98 **A** **Where do you hear *d*? Where do you hear *w*?**

Dd	
beginning ▪▫▫	1. ⓓA Y
middle ▫ⓓ▫	2. S T U ⓓ E N T
end ▫▫▪	3. C L O S E ⓓ

Ww	
beginning ▪▫▫	4. ⓦE E K
middle ▫ⓦ▫	5. N E ⓦP O R T
end ▫▫▪	6. N E ⓦ

Listening p. 98 **B** **Where do you hear *d*? Listen and check (✔).**

Dd	1.	2.	3.	4.	5.	6.
beginning ▪▫▫	✔					
middle ▫▪▫						
end ▫▫▪						

Listening p. 98 **C** **Where do you hear *w*? Listen and check (✔).**

Ww	1.	2.	3.	4.	5.	6.
beginning ▪▫▫						
middle ▫▪▫	✔					
end ▫▫▪						

D **Read the flyer. Circle *d* and *w*.**

English Classes
Davis Adult School
Monday, Wednesday, Friday
6:30 p.m. to 8:30 p.m.

E **Make a flyer for your English class. Where is class? When is class? What time is class?**

Word Patterns with -*ay*

Listening p. 98 **A** **Look at the pictures. Listen and read the words.**

1.

day

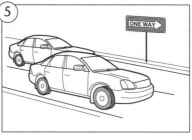
2.

MAY

May

3.

A, B, C

say

4.

pay

5.

ONE WAY

way

6.

hay

B **Read and complete the words.**

1. day   d _ay_
2. May   M ____
3. say   s ____

4. pay   p ____
5. way   w ____
6. hay   h ____

Listening p. 98 **C** **Listen and complete the words.**

1. _d_ ay
2. ___ ay

3. ___ ay
4. ___ ay

5. ___ ay
6. ___ ay

D **Write a sentence to remember the – *ay* sound.**

I pay for hay in May.

Your sentence

_____

_____

Cc and *CH/ch*

Listening p. 98 **A** Listen and number the pictures.

B Draw a line from the pictures to the words with *c* or *ch*.

cent   circle   city

check   chair   Charlie

Listening p. 98 **C** Listen and complete the words with *c* or *ch*.

1. _c_ ent   3. ___ ity   5. ___ air

2. ___ ircle   4. ___ eck   6. ___ arlie

D Write a word to remember *c*. Write a word to remember *ch*.

Cc
_____

CH/ch
_____

A Good Store

A **Read the story.**

Clothes Mart is a good store.

The clothes are good.

The prices are cheap.

B **Circle *yes* or *no*.**

1. Clothes Mart is a good store.	(yes)	no
2. Clothes Mart is a bad store.	yes	no
3. The clothes are not good.	yes	no
4. The clothes are good.	yes	no
5. The prices are cheap.	yes	no
6. The prices are not cheap.	yes	no

C **Write the *yes* sentences. Read the story to a partner.**

Clothes Mart is a good store.

_____

_____

D **Circle the periods (.) in the story. Underline *c* and *ch*.**

This/That and *These/Those*

A Look at the picture. Circle the sentence.

 1.

That book is $15.   This book is $15.

 2.

This book is $15.   That book is $15.

 3.

Those books are cheap.   These books are cheap.

 4.

Those books are cheap.   These books are cheap.

 5.

These books are cheap.   Those shoes are cheap.

B Write the circled sentences on your paper.

C Cut apart the cards. Make sentences.

THIS	THESE	THAT
THOSE	BOOK	BOOKS
IS	ARE	CHEAP.

How, Much, The, It's

A **Read the conversation.**

Cindy: <u>How</u> much is the book?
Mr. Chavez: It's $35.

B **Underline these words in the conversation.**

~~How~~	much	the	It's

C **Write the words.**

1. How _____How_____   3. much _____
2. the _____   4. It's _____

D **Circle the sight words in the puzzle.**

P	S	D	Z	C	P	D	T
T	U	C	(H	O	W)	'S	H
H	Q	M	U	C	Z	X	O
E	M	U	C	H	M	N	S
R	V	W	M	U	P	'S	A
B	Q	I	T	'S	I	Q	E

Cc and *CH/ch*

Listening
p. 98 **A** **Listen for the sound of *c*. Listen for the sound of *ch*.**

Cc
1. <u>C</u> I R C L E
2. <u>C</u> I T Y
3. <u>C</u> E N T S

CH/ch
1. <u>CH</u> A I R
2. <u>CH</u> E C K
3. <u>CH</u> E A P

Listening
p. 98 **B** **Listen and check (✔) the sound you hear.**

	Cc	*CH/ch*
1.		✔
2.		
3.		
4.		
5.		
6.		

Listening
p. 98 **C** **Listen and circle the word you hear.**

1. (cent)   check
2. chair   circle
3. circle   city

4. Charlie   city
5. cheap   circle
6. city   check

D **Read the check. Circle *c* and *ch*.**

CHARLIE SMITH   230
1256 Center Ave
Boston, MA 02108   DATE March 3, 2009

PAY TO THE
ORDER OF _____ Cindy's Candy Store _____ $ 23.56

Twenty-three and 56/100 _____ DOLLARS

                                              Charlie Smith

000500321 ⑆6790046 33⑆   6721786988⑈ _____

E **Make a check. Write the check to a store in your community that begins with *C* or *Ch*.**

Word Patterns with -*ent*

Listening p. 98 **A** **Look at the pictures. Listen and read the words.**

① cent

② dent

③ rent

④ tent

⑤ vent

⑥ Kent

B **Read and complete the words.**

1. cent   c _ent_   4. tent   t ____
2. dent   d ____   5. vent   v ____
3. rent   r ____   6. Kent   K ____

Listening p. 98 **C** **Listen and complete the words.**

1. _c_ ent   3. ___ ent   5. ___ ent
2. ___ ent   4. ___ ent   6. ___ ent

D **Write a sentence to remember the –*ent* sound.**

Kent has a tent for rent.

Your sentence

_____

_____

Bb and *Gg*

 A **Listen and number the pictures.**

B **Draw a line from the pictures to the words with *b* or *g*.**

boy   baby   birthday   book

girl   go   goodbye   gas

 C **Listen and complete the words with *b* or *g*.**

1. <u>b</u> oy   4. ___ ook   7. ___ oodbye

2. ___ aby   5. ___ irl   8. ___ as

3. ___ irthday   6. ___ o

D **Write a word to remember *b*. Write a word to remember *g*.**

Bb

_____

Gg

_____

My Children

A Read the story.

These are my children.

This is my son.

He's seven years old.

This is my daughter.

She's ten years old.

B Circle *yes* or *no*.

1. These are my children.		yes	no
2. This is my son.		yes	no
3. This is my teacher.		yes	no
4. He's seven years old.		yes	no
5. He's six years old.		yes	no
6. This is my daughter.		yes	no
7. This is my teacher.		yes	no
8. She's ten years old.		yes	no

C Write the *yes* sentences. Read the story to a partner.

  These are my children.

_____

_____

_____

_____

D Circle the periods (.) in the story. Underline the numbers.

Possessive Adjectives/Simple Present

A Look at the picture. Circle the sentence or sentences.

1 My daughter lives in New York.   My son lives in New York.

2 My son lives in Mexico.   My daughter lives in Mexico.

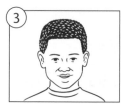

3 This is my son. His name is Greg.   This is my daughter. Her name is Gloria.

4 This is my father and mother. Their names are Mr. and Mrs. Garcia.   This is my sister. Her name is Galina.

5 This is my father and mother. They live in Kansas.   This is my mother. She lives in Kansas.

B Write the circled sentences on your paper.

C Cut apart the cards. Make sentences.

MY	DAUGHTER	SON
LIVES	FATHER AND MOTHER	LIVE
IN MEXICO.	HER	HIS

Who, That, Daughter, Her

A **Read the conversation.**

Gloria: Who is that?
Barbara: That is my daughter.
Gloria: What is her name?
Barbara: Her name is Patricia.

B **Underline these words in the conversation.**

~~Who~~	That	daughter	her

C **Write the words.**

1. Who _____Who_____   3. daughter _____

2. That _____   4. her _____

D **Complete the sentences. Write the words in the puzzle.**

_____Who_____ is _____ ?
     1   2

That is my _____.
                3

What is _____ name?
              4

Her name is Patricia.

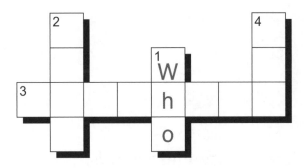

Bb and *Gg*

Listening p. 98 **A** **Listen for the sound of *b*. Listen for the sound of *g*.**

Bb
1. B O Y
2. B A B Y
3. B O O K

Gg
4. G I R L
5. G O
6. G A S

Listening p. 98 **B** **Listen and check (✔) the sound you hear.**

	b	*g*
1.		✔
2.		
3.		
4.		
5.		
6.		

Listening p. 98 **C** **Listen and circle the word you hear.**

1. (bus)   boy
2. bye   goodbye
3. birthday   goodbye
4. girl   birthday
5. bus   gas
6. book   good

D **Read the note. Circle *b* and *g*.**

> Mrs. Brown,
>   My family goes to Boston on Thursday.
> Galina needs her homework for the weekend.
>   Thank you,
>   Bob Garcia

E **Write a note from Mrs. Brown to Bob. Use these words.**

Mr. Garcia   homework   in her binder

Word Patterns with *-old*

A Look at the pictures. Listen and read the words.

Listening p. 98

1

2

3

old

cold

sold

4

5

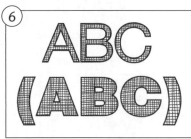
6

hold

gold

bold

B Read and complete the words.

1. old   old   4. hold   h ____
2. cold   c ____   5. gold   g ____
3. sold   s ____   6. bold   b ____

C Listen and complete the words.

Listening p. 98

1. old   3. ___ old   5. ___ old
2. ___ old   4. ___ old   6. ___ old

D Write a sentence to remember the *–old* sound.

Your sentence

_____

_____

The old, cold house sold.

Unit 6 Word Patterns with *-old* **59**

Ff and *Vv*

Listening p. 98 **A** Listen and number the pictures.

B Draw a line from the pictures to the words with *f* or *v*.

fruit	first name	four	fifty
vegetables	van	vent	verbs

Listening p. 98 **C** Listen and complete the words with *f* or *v*.

1. __f__ ruit
2. ___ irst name
3. ___ our

4. ___ ifty
5. ___ egetables
6. ___ an

7. ___ ent
8. ___ erbs

D Write a word to remember *f*. Write a word to remember *v*.

Ff

_____

Vv

_____

I Like Cheese

A **Read the story.**

I like cheese.

My husband likes beef.

My daughter likes chicken.

We all like rice.

B **Circle *yes* or *no*.**

1. I like cheese.	(yes)	no
2. I don't like cheese.	yes	no
3. My husband likes cheese.	yes	no
4. My husband likes beef.	yes	no
5. My daughter likes chicken.	yes	no
6. My daughter likes cheese.	yes	no
7. We all like rice.	yes	no
8. We all like pork.	yes	no

C **Write the *yes* sentences. Read the story to a partner.**

  I like cheese.

_____

_____

_____

D **Circle the periods (.) in the story. Underline the foods.**

Negative Statements

A Look at the picture. Circle the sentence.

She likes chicken.   She doesn't like chicken.

He likes chicken.   He doesn't like chicken.

They don't like fruit.   They like fruit.

He needs rice.   He doesn't need rice.

She needs chicken.   She doesn't need chicken.

B Write the circled sentences on your paper.

C Cut apart the cards. Make sentences.

HE	SHE	THEY
LIKE	DON'T	DOESN'T
FRUIT.	VEGETABLES.	LIKES

Me, Need, Here, Go

A **Read the conversation.**

Flor: Can you help <u>me</u>?
Clerk: Yes.
Flor: I need apples.
Clerk: Here you go.

B **Underline these words in the conversation.**

~~me~~	need	Here	go

C **Write the words.**

1. me _____me_____   3. here _____

2. need _____   4. go _____

D **Circle the sight words.**

M	A	E	L	H	N	I
B	H	E	R	E	E	K
V	I	T	Q	R	E	J
X	M	U	N	Z	D	M
C	S	L	G	O	G	E
N	E	E	B	R	V	O

Ff and *Vv*

Listening p. 99 **A** **Where do you hear *f*? Where do you hear *v*?**

Ff	
beginning ■□□	1. (F) I N E
middle ■■□	2. C A L I (F) O R N I A
end □■□	3. Y O U R S E L (F)

Vv	
beginning ■□□	4. (V) E G E T A B L E
middle ■■□	5. D I (V) O R C E D
end □□■	6. F I (V) E

Listening p. 99 **B** **Where do you hear *f*? Listen and check (✔).**

Ff	1.	2.	3.	4.	5.	6.
beginning ■□□	✔					
middle ■■□						
end □■□						

Listening p. 99 **C** **Where do you hear *v*? Listen and check (✔).**

Vv	1.	2.	3.	4.	5.	6.
beginning ■□□						
middle ■■□	✔					
end □■□						

D **Read the shopping list. Circle *f* and *v*.**

> fruit
> vegetable soup
> coffee
> 1 box of tea
> roast beef

E **Make a shopping list. Use words with *f* and *v*.**

Word Patterns with -*ice*

Listening p. 99 **A** **Look at the pictures. Listen and read the words.**

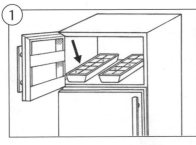
① ice

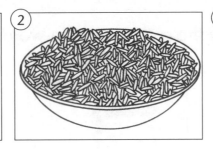
② rice

③ price

④ slice

⑤ mice

⑥ dice

B **Read and complete the words.**

1. ice   ice
2. rice   r ____
3. price pr ____

4. slice sl ____
5. mice   m ____
6. dice   d ____

Listening p. 99 **C** **Listen and complete the words.**

1. ice
2. ___ ice

3. ___ ice
4. ___ ice

5. ___ ice
6. ___ ice

D **Write a sentence to remember the –*ice* sound.**

The mice like rice, not ice.

Your sentence

_____

_____

Hh, *Ss*, and *SH/sh*

Listening p. 99 **A** **Listen and number the pictures.**

B **Draw a line from the pictures to the words with *h, s,* or *sh*.**

hand	head	husband	Hana
sick	son	shirt	shoes

Listening p. 99 **C** **Listen and complete the words with *h, s,* or *sh*.**

1. <u>h</u> and
2. ___ ead
3. ___ usband

4. ___ ana
5. ___ ick
6. ___ on

7. ___ irt
8. ___ oes

D **Write a word to remember *h*. Write words to remember *SH/ sh*.**

Hh
_____

SH/sh
_____

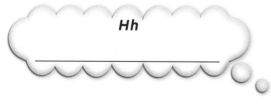

My Family Is Sick

A **Read the story.**

My family is sick.

My daughter has a cold.

My son has an earache.

My husband has a sore throat.

I have a headache.

B **Circle *yes* or *no*.**

1. My family is sick.	(yes)	no
2. My daughter has an earache.	yes	no
3. My daughter has a cold.	yes	no
4. My son has a headache.	yes	no
5. My son has an earache.	yes	no
6. My husband has a sore throat.	yes	no
7. My husband has a headache.	yes	no
8. I have a headache.	yes	no

C **Write the *yes* sentences. Read the story to a partner.**

My family is sick.

_____

_____

_____

_____

D **Circle the periods (.) in the story. Underline the health problems.**

Have and *Has*

A **Look at the picture. Circle the sentence.**

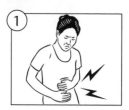

1   She has an earache.   She has a stomachache.

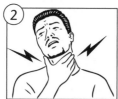

2   He has a sore throat.   They have sore throats.

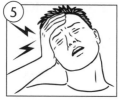

3   I have the flu.   They have the flu.

4   I have a cough.   They have a cough.

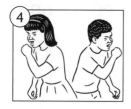

5   She has a headache.   He has a headache.

B **Write the circled sentences on your paper.**

C **Cut apart the cards. Make sentences.**

HE	SHE	THEY
HAVE	HAS	YOU
I	A HEADACHE.	THE FLU.

Hello, This, What, Stomachache

A **Read the conversation.**

Receptionist: <u>Hello</u>. Downtown Clinic.
Hana:　　　　 This is Hana Smith.
　　　　　　　　I need to see the doctor.
Receptionist: What is the matter?
Hana:　　　　 I have a stomachache.

B **Underline these words in the conversation.**

~~Hello~~	This	What	stomachache

C **Write the words.**

1. Hello ___Hello___
2. This _____

3. What _____
4. stomachache _____

D **Complete the sentences. Write the words in the puzzle.**

_____. Downtown Clinic.
₁

_____ is Hana Smith.
₂

_____ is the matter?
₃

I have a _____.
　　　　　　 4

Hh, Ss, and *SH/sh*

Listening
p. 99 **A** Listen for the sound of *h*. Listen for the sound of *s*. Listen for the sound of *sh*.

Hh	*Ss*	*SH/sh*
1. H E A D	3. S O N	5. S H I R T
2. H A N D	4. S I C K	6. S H O E

Listening
p. 99 **B** Listen and check (✔) the sound you hear.

	Hh	*Ss*	*SH/sh*
1.	✔		
2.			
3.			
4.			
5.			
6.			

Listening
p. 99 **C** Circle the word you hear.

1. (head)   sick   4. six   shoes
2. shirt   sick   5. son   she
3. hello   shoes   6. stomachache   headache

D Read the medicine label. Circle *s* and *sh*.

E Make a medicine label for headache tablets. Use words with *h, s,* and *sh*.

Word Patterns with -*eet*

Listening
p. 99

A **Look at the pictures. Listen and read the words.**

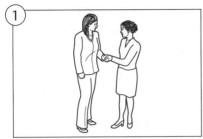

1. meet

2. greet

3. street (Hill St.)

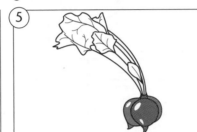

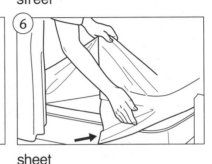

4. feet

5. beet

6. sheet

B **Read and complete the words.**

1. meet   m <u>eet</u>

2. greet   gr ____

3. street str ____

4. feet   f ____

5. beet   b ____

6. sheet   sh ____

Listening
p. 99

C **Listen and complete the words.**

1. <u>m</u> eet

2. ___ eet

3. ___ eet

4. ___ eet

5. ___ eet

6. ___ eet

D **Write a sentence to remember the – *eet* sound.**

SIXTH STREET   HELLO.

We meet and greet on the street.

Your sentence

_____

_____

Yy, Ww, and *WH/wh*

 A **Listen and number the pictures.**

B **Draw a line from the pictures to the words with *y, w,* or *wh*.**

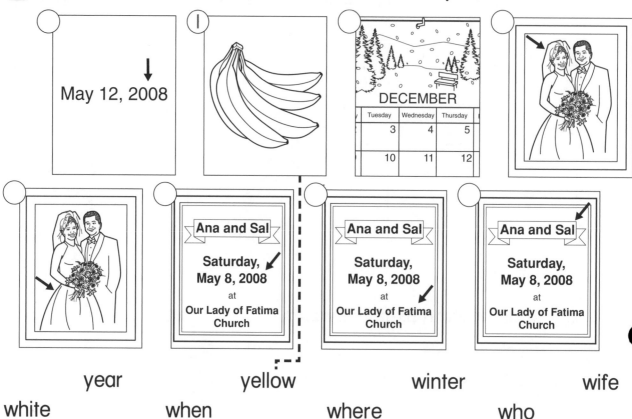

May 12, 2008

DECEMBER

Tuesday	Wednesday	Thursday
3	4	5
10	11	12

Ana and Sal
Saturday,
May 8, 2008
at
Our Lady of Fatima
Church

Ana and Sal
Saturday,
May 8, 2008
at
Our Lady of Fatima
Church

Ana and Sal
Saturday,
May 8, 2008
at
Our Lady of Fatima
Church

year   yellow   winter   wife

white   when   where   who

 C **Listen and complete the words with *y, w,* or *wh*.**

1. _y_ ear   4. ___ ife   7. ___ ere

2. ___ ellow   5. ___ ite   8. ___ o

3. ___ inter   6. ___ en

D **Write a word to remember *y*. Write words to remember *y* and *wh*.**

Yy
_____

WH/wh
_____

It's July

A **Read the story.**

It's July.

I'm wearing white shorts.

I'm wearing a red T-shirt.

I'm wearing a blue cap.

B **Circle *yes* or *no*.**

1. It's July.	(yes)	no
2. It's May.	yes	no
3. I'm wearing white shorts.	yes	no
4. I'm wearing yellow shorts.	yes	no
5. I'm wearing a red T-shirt.	yes	no
6. I'm wearing a white T-shirt.	yes	no
7. I'm wearing a blue cap.	yes	no
8. I'm wearing a red cap.	yes	no

C **Write the *yes* sentences. Read the story to a partner.**

It's July.

_____

_____

_____

D **Circle the periods (.) in the story. Underline the colors.**

Present Continuous

A **Look at the picture. Circle the sentence.**

She is wearing a shirt.   〔 He is wearing a shirt. 〕

She is wearing a skirt.   She is wearing a dress.

He is wearing
black shoes.   She is wearing
black shoes.

They are wearing
white coats.   I am wearing a
white coat.

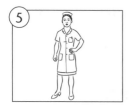
She is wearing a white
coat and shoes.   They are wearing white
coats and shoes.

B **Write the circled sentences on your paper.**

C **Cut apart the cards. Make sentences.**

WHITE COATS.	BLACK SHOES.	SHE
HE	IS	ARE
THEY	WEARING	A

Looking, For, Size, Small

A **Read the conversation.**

Yen: I'm <u>looking</u> for a T-shirt.
Clerk: What size?
Yen: Small.

B **Underline these words in the conversation.**

<s>looking</s>	for	size	Small

C **Write the words.**

1. looking ____looking____   3. size _____

2. for _____   4. Small _____

D **Complete the sentences. Write the words in the puzzle.**

I'm ____looking____ _____ a T-shirt.
            1   2

What _____?
            3

_____.
      4

Yy, Ww, and WH/wh

 A **Listen for the sound of *y*. Listen for the sound of *w*. Listen for the sound of *wh*.**

Yy		Ww		WH/wh	
1. <u>Y</u> E L L O W		3. <u>W</u> I N T E R		5. <u>WH</u> I T E	
2. <u>Y</u> E S		4. <u>W</u> I F E		6. <u>WH</u> E R E	

 B **Listen and check (✔) the sound you hear.**

	y	*w*	*wh*
1.		✔	
2.			
3.			
4.			
5.			
6.			

C **Listen and circle the word you hear.**

1. (year)   when   4. winter   when
2. year   where   5. yellow   white
3. wife   white   6. who   yellow

D **Read the weather page from the newspaper. Circle *w* and *wh*.**

E **Make a weather page for Wednesday and Thursday. Use words with *y*, *w*, and *wh*.**

Word Patterns with -*ue*

  **A** Look at the pictures. Listen and read the words.

1

blue

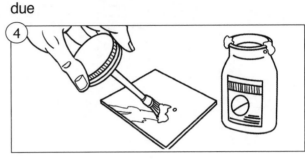

2 **KANSAS GAS COMPANY**

Amount Due: $32.89

due

3

SUE

Sue

4

glue

B Read and complete the words.

1. blue   bl __ue__

2. due   d ____

3. Sue   S ____

4. glue   gl ____

 C Listen and complete the words.

1. __bl__ ue

2. ___ ue

3. ___ ue

4. ___ ue

D Write a sentence to remember the –*ue* sound.

Sue puts glue on blue paper.

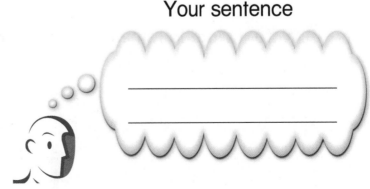

Your sentence

_____

_____

Ll and *Pp*

A Listen and number the pictures.

Listening p. 99

B Draw a line from the pictures to the words with *l* or *p*.

laundromat   library   lamp   list

post office   park   pencil   paper

C Listen and complete the words with *l* or *p*.

Listening p. 99

1. __l__ aundromat
2. ___ ibrary
3. ___ amp

4. ___ ist
5. ___ ost office
6. ___ ark

7. ___ encil
8. ___ aper

D Write a word to remember *l*. Write a word to remember *p*.

Ll

_____

Pp

_____

My Apartment Building

A Read the story.

My apartment building is on Pine Street.

There's a restaurant next to the laundromat.

There's a park on the corner.

I go to the park on Saturdays.

B Circle *yes* or *no*.

1. My apartment building is on Pine Street.   (yes)   no
2. My apartment is on Park Street.   yes   no
3. There's a restaurant next to the police station.   yes   no
4. There's a restaurant next to the laundromat.   yes   no
5. There's a library on the corner.   yes   no
6. There's a park on the corner.   yes   no
7. I go to the park on Saturdays.   yes   no
8. I go to the park on Sundays.   yes   no

C Write the *yes* sentences. Read the story to a partner.

My apartment building is on Pine Street.

_____

_____

_____

D Circle the periods (.) in the story. Underline the places.

There is, There are

A Look at the picture. Circle the sentence.

1. 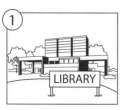   (There is a library.)   There are two libraries.

2. 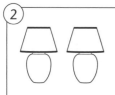   There is a lamp.   There are two lamps.

3. 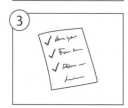   There is a list.   There are two lists.

4.    There is a pencil.   There are two pencils.

5.    There is a park.   There are two parks.

B Write the circled sentences on your paper.

C Cut apart the cards. Make sentences.

THERE	IS	ARE
PARKS.	A	PENCIL.
TWO	PARK.	PENCILS.

Where, Next, You, Welcome

A **Read the conversation.**

Lila: Excuse me. <u>Where</u> is the library?
Paul: It's next to the park.
Lila: Thank you.
Paul: You're welcome.

B **Underline these words in the conversation.**

~~Where~~	next	you	welcome

C **Write the words.**

1. Where _____Where_____　　　3. you _____

2. next _____　　　4. welcome _____

D **Complete the sentences. Write the words in the puzzle.**

Excuse me. _____Where_____ is the library?
　　　　　　　　　　1

It's _____ to the park.
　　　　2

Thank _____.
　　　　　　3

You're _____.
　　　　　4

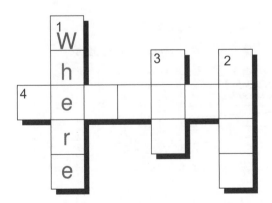

Ll and *Pp*

A **Where do you hear *l*? Where do you hear *p*?**
Listening p. 100

Ll	
beginning ■□□	1. (L) I B R A R Y
middle □■□	2. A M B U (L) A N C E
end □□■	3. H O S P I T A (L)

Pp	
beginning ■□□	4. (P) O L I C E
middle □■□	5. H O S (P) I T A L
end □□■	6. M A (P)

B **Where do you hear *l*? Listen and check (✔).**
Listening p. 100

Ll	1.	2.	3.	4.	5.	6.
beginning ■□□	✔					
middle □■□						
end □□■						

C **Where do you hear *p*? Listen and check (✔).**
Listening p. 100

Pp	1.	2.	3.	4.	5.	6.
beginning ■□□						
middle □■□						
end □□■	✔					

D **Read the signs. Circle *l* and *p*.**

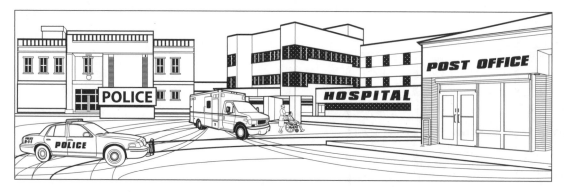

E **Make a list of community signs with *l* or *p*.**

Word Patterns with -*ot*

Listening p. 100 **A** **Look at the pictures. Listen and read the words.**

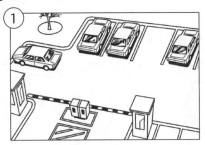 parking lot
 pot
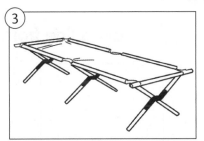 cot

 tot
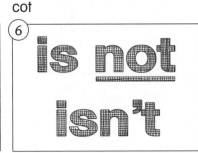 hot

is not
isn't
not

B **Read and complete the words.**

1. lot   l _ot_
2. pot   p ___
3. cot   c ___

4. tot   t ___
5. hot   h ___
6. not   n ___

Listening p. 100 **C** **Listen and complete the words.**

1. _l_ ot
2. ___ ot
3. ___ ot
4. ___ ot
5. ___ ot
6. ___ ot

D **Write a sentence to remember the –*ot* sound.**

The pot is not hot.

Your sentence

_____
_____

Kk and *Rr*

 A Listen and number the pictures.

Listening p. 100

B Draw a line from the pictures to the words with *k* or *r*.

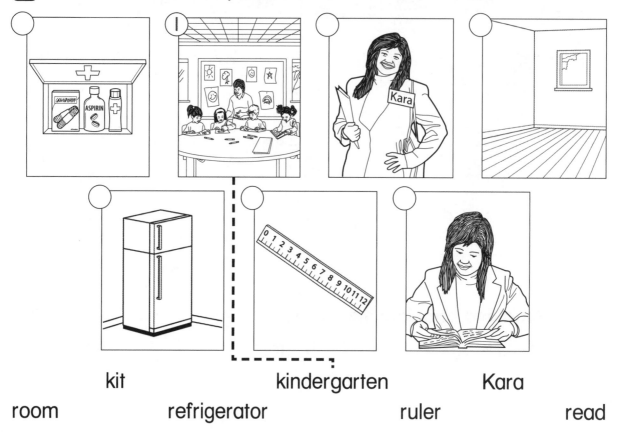

kit   kindergarten   Kara

room   refrigerator   ruler   read

Listening p. 100 **C** Listen and complete the words with *k* or *r*.

1. _k_ it   4. ___ oom   7. ___ ead

2. ___ indergarten   5. ___ efrigerator

3. ___ ara   6. ___ uler

D Write a word to remember *k*. Write a word to remember *r*.

Kk   Rr

_____   _____

This Is My Home

A Read the story.

This is my home.

There is one bedroom and one bathroom.

There is a red sofa in the living room.

There are two windows above the sofa.

I like my home.

B Circle *yes* or *no*.

1. This is my home.	(yes)	no
2. There is one bedroom and one bathroom.	yes	no
3. There are two bedrooms and one bathroom.	yes	no
4. There is a blue sofa in the living room.	yes	no
5. There is a red sofa in the living room.	yes	no
6. There is one window above the sofa.	yes	no
7. There are two windows above the sofa.	yes	no
8. I like my home.	yes	no

C Write the *yes* sentences. Read the story to a partner.

This is my home.

_____

_____

_____

_____

D Circle the periods (.) in the story. Underline the rooms.

Possessives

A Look at the picture. Circle the sentence.

    ⟨Kara's house is small.⟩   Kofi's house is small.

    Rosa's house is big.   Mr. Reza's house is big.

    Rosa's table is in   Rosa's table is in
    the living room.   the kitchen.

    Joe's TV is in   Joe's TV is in the
    the kitchen.   living room.

    Kofi's bed is small.   Kofi's bed is big.

B Write the circled sentences on your paper.

C Cut apart the cards. Make sentences.

KARA'S	ROSA'S	KOFI'S
SMALL.	BED	KITCHEN
BIG.	IS	TV.

There, Apartment, Many, Two

A **Read the conversation.**

Kofi: Is <u>there</u> an apartment for rent?
Manager: Yes.
Kofi: How many bedrooms are there?
Manager: Two.

B **Underline these words in the conversation.**

~~there~~	apartment	many	Two

C **Write the words.**

1. there _____there_____

3. many _____

2. apartment _____

4. Two _____

D **Complete the sentences. Write the words in the puzzle.**

Is _____there_____ an _____ for rent?
      1   2
Yes.

How _____ bedrooms are there?
       3

_____.
    4

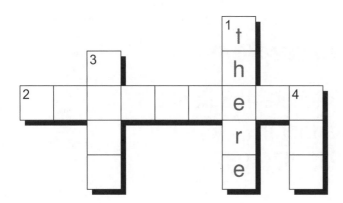

Kk and *Rr*

Listening p. 100 **A** Where do you hear *k*? Where do you hear *r*?

Kk	
beginning ▪▫▫	1. Ⓚ I T
middle ▫▪▫	2. B O O Ⓚ S T O R E
end ▫▫▪	3. B O O Ⓚ

Rr	
beginning ▪▫▫	4. Ⓡ O O M
middle ▫▪▫	5. B E D Ⓡ O O M
end ▫▫▪	6. C H A I Ⓡ

Listening p. 100 **B** Where do you hear *k*? Listen and check (✔).

Kk	1.	2.	3.	4.	5.	6.
beginning ▪▫▫	✔					
middle ▫▪▫						
end ▫▫▪						

Listening p. 100 **C** Where do you hear *r*? Listen and check (✔).

Rr	1.	2.	3.	4.	5.	6.
beginning ▪▫▫	✔					
middle ▫▪▫						
end ▫▫▪						

D Read the housing ad. Circle *k* and *r*.

Apartment for Rent

2BR/1BA apt. Lg. kitchen, 453 Kent St.
$700 a month
Call Karen 555-879-0874

E Make a housing ad for an apartment. Use words with *r* and *k*.

Word Patterns with -*ug*

Listening p. 100 **A** Look at the pictures. Listen and read the words.

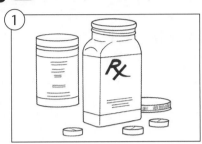
1

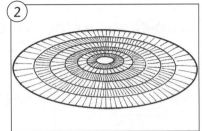
2

3

drug

rug

bug

4

5

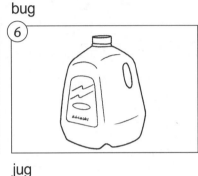
6

hug

mug

jug

B Read and complete the words.

1. drug   dr _ug_

2. rug   r ____

3. bug   b ____

4. hug   h ____

5. mug   m ____

6. jug   j ____

Listening p. 100 **C** Listen and complete the words.

1. _dr_ ug

2. ___ ug

3. ___ ug

4. ___ ug

5. ___ ug

6. ___ ug

D Write a sentence to remember the –*ug* sound.

Your sentence

_____

_____

The bug is on the mug on the rug.

Jj and Zz

A Listen and number the pictures.
Listening p. 100

B Draw a line from the pictures to the words with *j* or *z*.

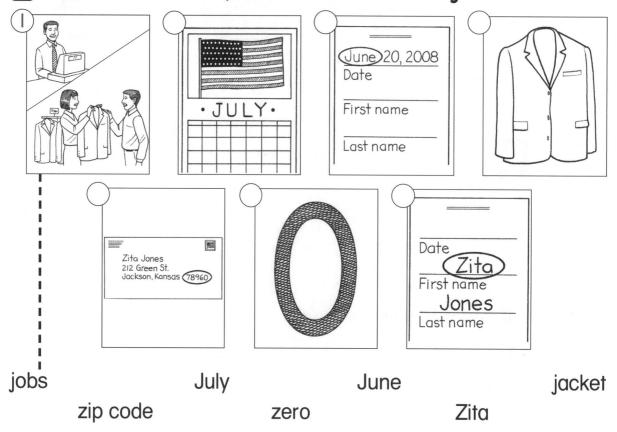

jobs   July   June   jacket

zip code   zero   Zita

Listening p. 100
C Listen and complete the words with *j* or *z*.

1. _j_ obs   4. ___ acket   7. ___ ita
2. ___ uly   5. ___ ip code   6. ___ ero
3. ___ une

D Write a word to remember *j*. Write a word to remember *z*.

Jj

Zz

Jobs

A **Read the story.**

My brother is a mechanic.

He can fix cars.

My friend is a truck driver.

She can drive trucks.

I want a job.

B **Circle *yes* or *no*.**

1. My brother is a mechanic.	(yes)	no
2. He can fix cars.	yes	no
3. He can't fix cars.	yes	no
4. My friend is a secretary.	yes	no
5. My friend is a truck driver.	yes	no
6. She can use a computer.	yes	no
7. She can drive trucks.	yes	no
8. I want a job.	yes	no

C **Write the *yes* sentences. Read the story to a partner.**

My brother is a mechanic.

_____

_____

_____

D **Circle the periods (.) in the story. Underline the jobs and the job skills.**

Can and *Can't*

A Look at the picture. Circle the sentence.

 She can drive a truck.   He can drive a truck.

 She can use a computer.   He can use a computer.

She can't fix cars.   He can't fix cars.

 Can he fix computers?   Can she fix computers?
Yes, he can.   Yes, she can.

 Can she fix cars?   Can she fix cars?
Yes, she can.   No, she can't.

B Write the circled sentences on your paper.

C Cut apart the cards. Make sentences.

SHE	I	HE
CAN	CAN'T	FIX CARS.
THEY	YOU	FIX CARS?

Use, Computer, Work, Evening

A **Read the conversation.**

John: Can you <u>use</u> a computer?
Zita: Yes, I can.
John: Can you work in the evening?
Zita: Yes, I can.

B **Underline these words in the conversation.**

~~use~~	computer	work	evening

C **Write the words.**

1. use _____use_____   3. work _____

2. computer _____   4. evening _____

D **Complete the sentences. Write the words in the puzzle.**

Can you _____use_____ a _____?
                 1   2
Yes I can.

Can you _____ in the _____?
                 3   4
Yes I can.

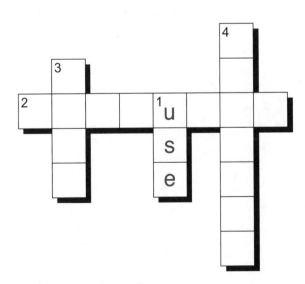

Jj and *Zz*

Listening
p. 100 **A** Listen for the sound of *j*. Listen for the sound of *z*.

Jj
1. J O B
2. J U L Y
3. J A C K E T

Zz
1. Z I P C O D E
2. Z E R O
3. S I Z E

Listening
p. 100 **B** Listen and check (✔) the sound you hear.

	Jj	*Zz*
1.	✔	
2.		
3.		
4.		
5.		
6.		

Listening
p. 100 **C** Listen and circle the word you hear.

1. jacket (Zita)
2. zero   job
3. July   zero

4. June   zero
5. zip code jacket
6. June   July

D Read the job ad. Circle *j* and *z*.

Need a summer job?
CASHIER
PT, M-W-F evenings, June-July,
Call Zita at Clothes Mart, 555-789-0003.

E Make a job ad for a bus driver. Use words with *j* and *z*.

Word Patterns with -ob

Listening p. 100 **A** Look at the pictures. Listen and read the words.

job

Bob

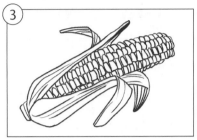

cob

rob

sob

B Read and complete the words.

1. job   j _ob_

2. Bob   B ___

3. cob   c ___

4. rob   r ___

5. sob   s ___

Listening p. 100 **C** Listen and complete the words.

1. _j_ ob

2. ___ ob

3. ___ ob

4. ___ ob

5. ___ ob

D Write a sentence to remember the –ob sound.

Bob sobs on the job.

Your sentence

_____

_____

Pre-unit The First Step

The Alphabet and You
page 20

A

A
B
C
D
E
F
G
H
I
J
K
L
M
N
O
P
Q
R
S
T
U
V
W
X
Y
Z

Letter Listening page 21
A

Number 1   t
Number 2   n
Number 3   s
Number 4   p
Number 5   i
Number 6   b
Number 7   c
Number 8   l
Number 9   b
Number 10   g
Number 11   y
Number 12   d

B

Number 1   a
Number 2   j
Number 3   n
Number 4   h
Number 5   e
Number 6   k
Number 7   u
Number 8   i
Number 9   b

Number 10   o
Number 11   p
Number 12   s

C

Number 1   s
Number 2   e
Number 3   r
Number 4   a
Number 5   c
Number 6   o
Number 7   n
Number 8   i

D

Number 1 pen, P-E-N
Number 2 book, B-O-O-K
Number 3 chair, C-H-A-I-R
Number 4 men, M-E-N
Number 5 clock, C-L-O-C-K
Number 6 desk, D-E-S-K

More Letter Listening page 22
A

Number 1   Y
Number 2   E
Number 3   C
Number 4   M
Number 5   B
Number 6   P
Number 7   L

B

Number 1   G
Number 2   I
Number 3   H
Number 4   E
Number 5   T
Number 6   V
Number 7   W
Number 8   A
Number 9   Z

C

Number 1   T-W-O
Number 2   F-I-V-E
Number 3   S-E-V-E-N
Number 4   O-N-E
Number 5   T-H-R-E-E
Number 6   T-E-N
Number 7   E-I-G-H-T

Number Listening page 23
A

a. zero
b. one
c. two
d. three
e. four
f. five

g. six
h. seven
i. eight
j. nine
k. ten

B

a. seven
b. five
c. two
d. six
e. one
f. four
g. three-zero-three
h. five-five-two
i. nine-one-seven
j. one-eight-nine

C

a. two-three-five—six-five-five-two
b. four-six-three—three-one-nine-four
c. five-eight-nine—four-seven-seven-one
d. two-zero-six—six-zero-two-one
e. nine-nine-two—three-four-two-eight
f. six-eight-four—nine-two-zero-seven

Unit 1 Nice to Meet You

Lesson 1 page 24
A

Number 1   count
Number 2   clock
Number 3   close
Number 4   say
Number 5   student
Number 6   sign

C

Number 1   clock
Number 2   count
Number 3   close
Number 4   student
Number 5   say
Number 6   sign

Lesson 5 page 28
A

Listen for the sound of *c*.
Number 1   clock
Number 2   close
Number 3   count
Listen for the sound of *s*.
Number 1   say
Number 2   student
Number 3   sign

B

Number 1	count
Number 2	close
Number 3	student
Number 4	say
Number 5	clock
Number 6	sign

C

Number 1	student
Number 2	clock
Number 3	sign
Number 4	count
Number 5	say
Number 6	class

Review and expand page 29

A

Number 1	can
Number 2	man
Number 3	Dan
Number 4	fan
Number 5	pan
Number 6	van

C

Number 1	can
Number 2	van
Number 3	Dan
Number 4	fan
Number 5	pan
Number 6	man

Unit 2 How are you feeling?

Lesson 1 page 30

A

Number 1	ten
Number 2	tired
Number 3	teacher
Number 4	three
Number 5	thirsty
Number 6	they

C

Number 1	tired
Number 2	teacher
Number 3	ten
Number 4	thirsty
Number 5	they
Number 6	three

Lesson 5 page 34

A

Listen for the sound of *t*.

Number 1	tired
Number 2	teacher
Number 3	ten

Listen for the sound of *th*.

Number 4	thirsty
Number 5	they
Number 6	three

B

Number 1	tired
Number 2	they
Number 3	ten

Number 4	then
Number 5	three
Number 6	teacher

C

Number 1	tired
Number 2	three
Number 3	thirteen
Number 4	they
Number 5	ten
Number 6	two

Review and expand
page 35

A

Number 1	ad
Number 2	sad
Number 3	bad
Number 4	dad
Number 5	mad
Number 6	pad

C

Number 1	ad
Number 2	sad
Number 3	bad
Number 4	dad
Number 5	mad
Number 6	pad

Unit 3 What time is it?

Lesson 1 page 36

A

Number 1	midnight
Number 2	morning
Number 3	men
Number 4	man
Number 5	noon
Number 6	night
Number 7	nine
Number 8	notebook

C

Number 1	morning
Number 2	man
Number 3	men
Number 4	midnight
Number 5	night
Number 6	noon
Number 7	notebook
Number 8	nine

Lesson 5 page 40

A

Mm: M is the beginning sound in *man*. Listen for *m*. Man.
M is the middle sound in *number*. Listen for *m*. Number
M is the end sound in *from*. Listen for *m*. From.
Nn: N is the beginning sound in *night*. Listen for *n*. Night.
N is the middle sound in *pencil*. Listen for *n*. Pencil.

N is the end sound in *pen*.
Listen for *n*. Pen.

B

Number 1	man
Number 2	classroom
Number 3	woman
Number 4	midnight
Number 5	morning
Number 6	number

C

Number 1	night
Number 2	open
Number 3	student
Number 4	notebook
Number 5	ten
Number 6	count

Review and expand
page 41

A

Number 1	it
Number 2	sit
Number 3	mitt
Number 4	kit
Number 5	hit
Number 6	fit

C

Number 1	it
Number 2	sit
Number 3	kit
Number 4	mitt
Number 5	hit
Number 6	fit

Unit 4 What day is it?

Lesson 1 page 42

A

Number 1	dictionary
Number 2	desk
Number 3	day
Number 4	Wednesday
Number 5	week
Number 6	weekend
Number 7	woman

C

Number 1	day
Number 2	desk
Number 3	dictionary
Number 4	week
Number 5	weekend
Number 6	Wednesday
Number 7	woman

Lesson 5 page 46

A

Dd: D is the beginning sound in *day*. Listen for *d*. Day.
D is the middle sound in *student*. Listen for *d*. Student.
D is the end sound in *closed*. Listen for *d*. Closed.
Ww: W is the beginning sound in *week*. Listen for *w*. Week.
W is the middle sound in *Newport*. Listen for *w*. Newport.
W is the end sound in *new*. Listen for *w*. New.

B

Number 1 desk
Number 2 tired
Number 3 midnight
Number 4 today
Number 5 sad
Number 6 weekend

C

Number 1 Newport
Number 2 Wednesday
Number 3 woman
Number 4 now
Number 5 weekend
Number 6 homework

Review and expand page 47

A

Number 1 day
Number 2 May
Number 3 say
Number 4 pay
Number 5 way
Number 6 hay

C

Number 1 day
Number 2 say
Number 3 hay
Number 4 May
Number 5 way
Number 6 pay

Unit 5 How much is it?

Lesson 1 page 48

A

Number 1 city
Number 2 circle
Number 3 cent
Number 4 Charlie
Number 5 check
Number 6 chair

C

Number 1 cent
Number 2 circle
Number 3 city
Number 4 check
Number 5 chair
Number 6 Charlie

Lesson 5 page 52

A

Listen for the sound of *c*.
Number 1 circle
Number 2 city
Number 3 cents
Listen for the sound of *ch*.
Number 4 chair
Number 5 check
Number 6 cheap

B

Number 1 chair
Number 2 cent
Number 3 circle
Number 4 Charlie
Number 5 check
Number 6 cheap

C

Number 1 cent
Number 2 chair
Number 3 city
Number 4 Charlie
Number 5 cheap
Number 6 check

Review and expand page 53

A

Number 1 cent
Number 2 dent
Number 3 rent
Number 4 tent
Number 5 vent
Number 6 Kent

C

Number 1 cent
Number 2 rent
Number 3 Kent
Number 4 tent
Number 5 dent
Number 6 vent

Unit 6 That's My Son

Lesson 1 page 54

A

Number 1 book
Number 2 baby
Number 3 birthday
Number 4 boy
Number 5 girl
Number 6 goodbye
Number 7 gas
Number 8 go

C

Number 1 boy
Number 2 baby
Number 3 birthday
Number 4 book
Number 5 girl
Number 6 go
Number 7 goodbye
Number 8 gas

Lesson 5 page 58

A

Listen for the sound of *b*.
Number 1 boy
Number 2 baby
Number 3 book
Listen for the sound of *g*.
Number 1 girl
Number 2 go
Number 3 gas

B

Number 1 girl
Number 2 birthday
Number 3 bus
Number 4 gas
Number 5 book
Number 6 good

C

Number 1 bus
Number 2 goodbye
Number 3 birthday
Number 4 girl
Number 5 gas
Number 6 book

Review and expand page 59

A

Number 1 old
Number 2 cold
Number 3 sold
Number 4 hold
Number 5 gold
Number 6 bold

C

Number 1 old
Number 2 sold
Number 3 bold
Number 4 gold
Number 5 hold
Number 6 cold

Unit 7 Do we need apples?

Lesson 1 page 60

A

Number 1 first name
Number 2 fruit
Number 3 four
Number 4 fifty
Number 5 verbs
Number 6 van
Number 7 vegetables
Number 8 vent

C

Number 1 fruit
Number 2 first name
Number 3 four
Number 4 fifty
Number 5 vegetables
Number 6 van
Number 7 vent
Number 8 verbs

Lesson 5 page 64

A

Ff: *F* is the beginning sound in *fine*. Listen for *f*. Fine.
F is the middle sound in *California*. Listen for *f*. California.
F is the end sound in *yourself*. Listen for *f*. Yourself.
Vv: *V* is the beginning sound in *vegetable*. Listen for *v*. Vegetable.
V is the middle sound in *divorced*. Listen for *v*. Divorced.
V is the end sound in *five*. Listen for *v*. Five.

B

Number 1   fruit
Number 2   information
Number 3   yourself
Number 4   first
Number 5   father
Number 6   beef

C

Number 1   November
Number 2   van
Number 3   vent
Number 4   expensive
Number 5   live
Number 6   seven

Review and expand
page 65

A

Number 1   ice
Number 2   rice
Number 3   price
Number 4   slice
Number 5   mice
Number 6   dice

C

Number 1   ice
Number 2   rice
Number 3   dice
Number 4   mice
Number 5   slice
Number 6   price

Unit 8 Take Two Tablets

Lesson 1 page 66

A

Number 1   Hana
Number 2   hand
Number 3   head
Number 4   husband
Number 5   son
Number 6   sick
Number 7   shoes
Number 8   shirt

C

Number 1   hand
Number 2   head
Number 3   husband

Number 4   Hana
Number 5   sick
Number 6   son
Number 7   shirt
Number 8   shoes

Lesson 5 page 70

A

Listen for the sound of *h*.
Number 1   head
Number 2   hand
Listen for the sound of *s*.
Number 3   son
Number 4   sick
Listen for the sound of *sh*.
Number 5   shirt
Number 6   shoe

B

Number 1   head
Number 2   sick
Number 3   shoe
Number 4   shirt
Number 5   son
Number 6   hand

C

Number 1   head
Number 2   sick
Number 3   shoes
Number 4   six
Number 5   she
Number 6   headache

Review and expand page 71

A

Number 1   meet
Number 2   greet
Number 3   street
Number 4   feet
Number 5   beet
Number 6   sheet

C

Number 1   meet
Number 2   feet
Number 3   greet
Number 4   beet
Number 5   sheet
Number 6   street

Unit 9 What size?

Lesson 1 page 72

A

Number 1   yellow
Number 2   year
Number 3   winter
Number 4   wife
Number 5   when
Number 6   who
Number 7   white
Number 8   where

C

Number 1   year
Number 2   yellow

Number 3   winter
Number 4   wife
Number 5   white
Number 6   when
Number 7   where
Number 8   who

Lesson 5 page 76

A

Listen for the sound of *y*.
Number 1   yellow
Number 2   yes
Listen for the sound of *w*.
Number 3   winter
Number 4   wife
Listen for the sound of *wh*.
Number 5   white
Number 6   where

B

Number 1   winter
Number 2   yellow
Number 3   wife
Number 4   white
Number 5   where
Number 6   year

C

Number 1   year
Number 2   where
Number 3   wife
Number 4   when
Number 5   yellow
Number 6   who

Review and expand
page 77

A

Number 1   blue
Number 2   due
Number 3   Sue
Number 4   glue

C

Number 1   blue
Number 2   ˑSue
Number 3   glue
Number 4   due

Unit 10 Where's the bank?

Lesson 1 page 78

A

Number 1   list
Number 2   lamp
Number 3   laundromat
Number 4   library
Number 5   paper
Number 6   park
Number 7   post office
Number 8   pencil

C

Number 1	laundromat
Number 2	library
Number 3	lamp
Number 4	list
Number 5	post office
Number 6	park
Number 7	pencil
Number 8	paper

Lesson 5 page 82

A

Ll: *L* is the beginning sound in *library*. Listen for *l*. Library.
L is the middle sound in *ambulance*. Listen for *l*. Ambulance.
L is the end sound in *hospital*. Listen for *l*. Hospital.
Pp: *P* is the beginning sound in *police*. Listen for *p*. Police.
P is the middle sound in *hospital*. Listen for *p*. Hospital.
P is the end sound in *map*. Listen for *p*. Map.

B

Number 1	list
Number 2	laundromat
Number 3	April
Number 4	July
Number 5	look
Number 6	middle

C

Number 1	cap
Number 2	pen
Number 3	happy
Number 4	pencil
Number 5	September
Number 6	lamp

Review and expand page 83

A

Number 1	parking lot
Number 2	pot
Number 3	cot
Number 4	tot
Number 5	hot
Number 6	not

C

Number 1	lot
Number 2	not
Number 3	cot
Number 4	pot
Number 5	hot
Number 6	tot

Unit 11 This Is My Home

Lesson 1 page 84

A

Number 1	kindergarten
Number 2	kit
Number 3	Kara
Number 4	room

Number 5	refrigerator
Number 6	read
Number 7	ruler

C

Number 1	kit
Number 2	kindergarten
Number 3	Kara
Number 4	room
Number 5	refrigerator
Number 6	ruler
Number 7	read

Lesson 5 page 88

A

Kk: *K* is the beginning sound in *kit*. Listen for *k*. Kit.
K is the middle sound in *bookstore*. Listen for *k*. Bookstore.
K is the end sound in *book*. Listen for *k*. Book.
Rr: *R* is the beginning sound in *room*. Listen for *r*. Room.
R is the middle sound in *bedroom*. Listen for *r*. Bedroom.
R is the end sound in *chair*. Listen for *r*. Chair.

B

Number 1	kitchen
Number 2	weekend
Number 3	look
Number 4	Kara
Number 5	park
Number 6	supermarket

C

Number 1	red
Number 2	bathroom
Number 3	rent
Number 4	apartment
Number 5	read
Number 6	car

Review and expand page 89

A

Number 1	drug
Number 2	rug
Number 3	bug
Number 4	hug
Number 5	mug
Number 6	jug

C

Number 1	drug
Number 2	mug
Number 3	rug
Number 4	bug
Number 5	jug
Number 6	hug

Unit 12 Yes, I can!

Lesson 1 page 90

A

Number 1	jobs
Number 2	jacket

Number 3	June
Number 4	July
Number 5	zip code
Number 6	Zita
Number 7	zero

C

Number 1	jobs
Number 2	July
Number 3	June
Number 4	jacket
Number 5	zip code
Number 6	zero
Number 7	Zita

Lesson 5 page 94

A

Listen for the sound of *j*.

Number 1	job
Number 2	July
Number 3	jacket

Listen for the sound of *z*.

Number 4	zip code
Number 5	zero
Number 6	size

B

Number 1	jacket
Number 2	zip code
Number 3	zero
Number 4	July
Number 5	June
Number 6	Zita

C

Number 1	Zita
Number 2	job
Number 3	July
Number 4	zero
Number 5	jacket
Number 6	June

Review and expand page 95

A

Number 1	job
Number 2	Bob
Number 3	cob
Number 4	rob
Number 5	sob

C

Number 1	job
Number 2	cob
Number 3	sob
Number 4	Bob
Number 5	rob

Pre-unit The First Step

Same and Different page 9

A

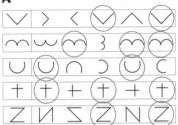

B

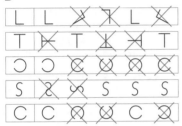

Circle the Number page 17

b. 9
c. 7
d. 4
e. 1
f. 10
g. 3
h. 2
i. 5
j. 6
k. 8

Write the Numbers page 18

B

b. 4, 7
c. 0, 2, 6, 9
d. 1,3, 5, 8, 10
e. 1, 2, 3, 4, 5, 6, 7, 8, 9, 10

Letter Listening page 21

B

2. j
3. n
4. h
5. e
6. k
7. u
8. i
9. b
10. o
11. p
12. s

C

2. e
3. r
4. a
5. c
6. o
7. n
8. i

D

2. book
3. chair
4. men
5. clock
6. desk

More Letter Listening page 22

B

2. I
3. H
4. E
5. T
6. V
7. W
8. A
9. Z

C

2. five
3. seven
4. one
5. three
6. ten
7. eight

Number Listening page 23

B

b. 5
c. 2
d. 6
e. 1
f. 4
g. 303
h. 552
i. 917
j. 189

C

b. 4 6 <u>3</u> – 3 1 9 <u>4</u>
c. 5 8 <u>9</u> – 4 <u>7</u> 7 <u>1</u>
d. <u>2</u> 0 <u>6</u> – 6 0 2 <u>1</u>
e. <u>9</u> <u>9</u> 2 – <u>3</u> 4 2 <u>8</u>
f. <u>6</u> 8 <u>4</u> – <u>9</u> 2 <u>0</u> 7

Unit 1 Nice to Meet You

Lesson 1 page 24

A

2. clock   5. student
3. close   6. sign
4. say

C

2. <u>c</u>ount   5. <u>s</u>ay
3. <u>c</u>lose   6. <u>s</u>ign
4. <u>s</u>tudent

D

Answers will vary.

Lesson 2 page 25

B

2. no   6. yes
3. yes   7. no
4. no   8. yes
5. no

C

My first name is Anita.
My last name is Salas.
I am a student.
My teacher is Kathy Rose.

D

My first name is <u>Anita</u>⊙
My last name is <u>Salas</u>⊙
I am a student⊙
My teacher is <u>Kathy Rose</u>⊙

Lesson 3 page 26

A

2. She is a student.
3. He is a student.
4. It is a pencil.
5. They are students.

B

1. I am a teacher.
2. She is a student.
3. He is a student.
4. It is a pencil.
5. They are students.

C

Answers will vary.

Lesson 4 page 27

B

Sal: Hi. <u>I</u> am Sal. What <u>is</u> your <u>name</u>?
Carla: <u>My</u> <u>name</u> <u>is</u> Carla.

C

2. is
3. name
4. my

D

B	N	A	M	Ⓘ	Y	S
X	Ⓝ	Ⓐ	Ⓜ	Ⓔ	X	N
T	T	M	D	R	M	R
C	Z	W	Ⓜ	Ⓨ	O	L
M	Ⓘ	B	J	P	R	P
O	Ⓢ	R	D	T	F	L

Lesson 5 page 28

B

2. c   5. c
3. s   6. s
4. s

C

2. clock   5. say
3. sign   6. class
4. count

D

Carr, Mrs. Benson, Sam, Clark

E

Answers will vary.

Review and expand page 29

B

2. man   5. pan
3. Dan   6. van
4. fan

C

2. van   5. pan
3. Dan   6. man
4. fan

D

Answers will vary.

Unit 2 How are you feeling?

Lesson 1 page 30

A

2. tired   5. thirsty
3. teacher   6. they
4. three

C

2. teacher   5. they
3. ten   6. three
4. thirsty

D

Answers will vary.

Lesson 2 page 31

B

2. no   6. no
3. no   7. no
4. yes   8. yes
5. yes

C

My name is Camille.
I am from Haiti.
Now I am in Dallas, Texas.
I am happy in Dallas.

D

My name is Camille.
I am from Haiti.
Now I am in Dallas, Texas.
I am happy in Dallas.

Lesson 3 page 32

A

2. He is tired.
3. They are thirsty.
4. She is not sad.
5. She is not happy. She's sick.

B

1. She is tired.
2. He is tired.
3. They are thirsty.
4. She is not sad.
5. She is not happy. She's sick.

C

Answers will vary.

Lesson 4 page 33

B

Tom: How are you feeling?
Teng: I'm fine. How are you feeling?
Tom: I'm sick.
Teng: Oh, I'm sorry.

C

1. are   3. fine
2. I'm   4. sorry

D

```
D S O R I R Y A
M (S O R R Y) P R
(A) F I N P D A T
(R) G (F I N E) I L
(E) I' A U Q I' B
X (I'M) D R O A M
```

Lesson 5 page 34

B

2. *th*   5. *th*
3. *t*   6. *t*
4. *th*

C

2. three   5. ten
3. thirteen   6. two
4. they

D

Tam, City, Adult, Third, Street, Austin, TX

E

Answers will vary.

Review and expand page 35

B

2. sad   5. pad
3. dad   6. bad
4. mad

C

2. sad   5. mad
3. bad   6. pad
4. dad

D

Answers will vary.

Unit 3 What time is it?

Lesson 1 page 36

A

2. morning   6. night
3. men   7. nine
4. man   8. notebook
5. noon

C

2. man   6. noon
3. men   7. notebook
4. midnight   8. nine
5. night

D

Answers will vary.

Lesson 2 page 37

B

2. no   6. yes
3. yes   7. yes
4. no   8. no
5. no

C

I go to the store at 8:00.
I go to the library at 9:30.
I go to school at 10:00.
I go to English class at 10:30.

D

I go to the store at 8:00.
I go to the library at 9:30.
I go to school at 10:00.
I go to English class at 10:30.

Lesson 3 page 38

A

2. Is he at school? Yes, he is.
3. Is it 9:00? Yes, it is.
4. Are they at home? Yes, they are.
5. Is she at the store? No, she isn't.

B

1. Is she at school? Yes, she is.
2. Is he at school? Yes, he is.
3. Is it 9:00? Yes, it is.
4. Are they at home? Yes, they are.
5. Is she at the store? No, she isn't.

C

Answers will vary.

Lesson 4 page 39

B

Marta: Excuse me. What time is it?
Min: It's 8:00.
Marta: Is the store open?
Min: No, it's not.

C

1. time   3. open
2. it   4. not

D

1. time   3. open
2. it   4. not

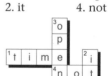

Lesson 5 page 40

B

2. end   5. beginning
3. middle   6. middle
4. beginning

C

2. end   5. end
3. middle   6. middle
4. beginning

D

(N)umber, (M)ain, (N)ewport, (M)apleton,
a.(m)., a.(m)., a.(m).

E

Answers will vary.

Review and expand page 41

B

2. <u>sit</u>   5. <u>hit</u>
3. <u>mitt</u>   6. <u>fit</u>
4. <u>kit</u>

C

2. sit   5. hit
3. kit   6. fit
4. mitt

D

Answers will vary.

Unit 4 What day is it?

Lesson 1 page 42

A

2. desk   5. week
3. day   6. weekend
4. Wednesday   7. woman

C

2. <u>d</u>esk   5. <u>w</u>eekend
3. <u>d</u>ictionary   6. <u>W</u>ednesday
4. <u>w</u>eek   7. <u>w</u>oman

D

Answers will vary.

Lesson 2 page 43

B

2. no   5. yes
3. no   6. no
4. yes

C

It's October.
Next month is November.
My birthday is in November.

D

It's <u>O</u>ctober⊙
Next month is <u>N</u>ovember⊙
My birthday is in <u>N</u>ovember⊙

Lesson 3 page 44

A

2. When is the English class?
3. What time is the English class?
4. The English class is at 6:30 p.m.
5. The English class is at Davis School.

B

1. Where is the English class?
2. When is the English class?
3. What time is the English class?
4. The English class is at 6:30 p.m.
5. The English class is at Davis School.

C

Answers will vary.

Lesson 4 page 45

B

Dara: Goodbye. <u>Have</u> a nice
      weekend.
Diana: <u>Thanks</u>. You, too. <u>See</u> you
      <u>Wednesday</u>.

C

1. have   3. see
2. thanks   4. Wednesday

D

Goodbye. <u>Have</u> a nice weekend.
<u>Thanks</u>. You, too.
<u>See</u> you <u>Wednesday</u>.

Lesson 5 page 46

B

2. end   5. end
3. middle   6. end
4. middle

C

2. beginning   5. beginning
3. beginning   6. middle
4. end

D

(D)avis A(d)ult School, Mon(d)ay,
We(d)nes(d)ay, Fri(d)ay

E

Answers will vary.

Review and expand page 47

B

2. <u>M</u>ay   5. <u>way</u>
3. <u>say</u>   6. <u>hay</u>
4. <u>pay</u>

C

2. <u>say</u>   5. <u>way</u>
3. <u>hay</u>   6. <u>pay</u>
4. <u>May</u>

D

Answers will vary.

Unit 5 How much is it?

Lesson 1 page 48

A

2. circle   5. check
3. cent   6. chair
4. Charlie

C

2. <u>c</u>ircle   5. <u>ch</u>air
3. <u>c</u>ity   6. <u>Ch</u>arlie
4. <u>ch</u>eck

D

Answers will vary.

Lesson 2 page 49

B

2. no   5. yes
3. no   6. no
4. yes

C

Clothes Mart is a good store.
The clothes are good.
The prices are cheap.

D

<u>C</u>lothes Mart is a good store⊙
The <u>c</u>lothes are good⊙
The pri<u>c</u>es are <u>ch</u>eap⊙

Lesson 3 page 50

A

2. This book is $15.
3. These books are cheap.
4. Those books are cheap.
5. Those shoes are cheap.

B

1. That book is $15.
2. This book is $15.
3. These books are cheap.
4. Those books are cheap.
5. Those shoes are cheap.

C

Answers will vary.

Lesson 4 page 51

B

Cindy: <u>How</u> <u>much</u> is <u>the</u> book?
Mr. Chavez: <u>It's</u> $35.

C

1. how   3. much
2. the   4. it's

D

```
P S D Z C P D T
T U C (H O W) 'S H
H Q M U C Z X O
E (M U C H) M N S
R V W M U P 'S A
B Q (I T 'S) I Q E
```

Lesson 5 page 52

B

2. c   5. ch
3. c   6. ch
4. ch

C

2. chair   5. cheap
3. city   6. check
4. Charlie

D

(Ch)arlie, (C)enter, Mar(ch), (C)indy's,
(C)andy, (Ch)arlie.

E

Answers will vary.

Review and expand Page 53

B

2. <u>dent</u>   5. <u>vent</u>
3. <u>rent</u>   6. <u>K</u>ent
4. <u>tent</u>

C

2. <u>r</u>ent   5. <u>d</u>ent
3. <u>K</u>ent   6. <u>v</u>ent
4. <u>t</u>ent

D

Answers will vary.

Unit 6 That's My Son

Lesson 1 page 54

A

2. baby   6. goodbye
3. birthday   7. gas
4. boy   8. go
5. girl

C

2. <u>baby</u>   6. go
3. <u>birthday</u>   7. goodbye
4. <u>book</u>   8. gas
5. girl

D

Answers will vary.

Lesson 2 page 55

B

2. yes   6. yes
3. no   7. no
4. yes   8. yes
5. no

C

These are my children.
This is my son.
He's seven years old.
This is my daughter.
She's ten years old.

D

These are my children⊙
This is my son⊙
He's <u>seven</u> years old⊙
This is my daughter⊙
She's <u>ten</u> years old⊙

Lesson 3 page 56

A

2. My son lives in Mexico.
3. This is my son. His name is Greg.
4. This is my father and mother. Their names are Mr. and Mrs. Garcia.
5. This is my mother. She lives in Kansas.

B

1. My daughter lives in New York.
2. My son lives in Mexico.
3. This is my son. His name is Greg.
4. This is my father and mother. Their names are Mr. and Mrs. Garcia.
5. This is my mother. She lives in Kansas.

C

Answers will vary.

Lesson 4 page 57

B

Gloria: <u>Who</u> is <u>that</u>?
Barbara: <u>That</u> is my <u>daughter</u>.
Gloria: What is <u>her</u> name?
Barbara: <u>Her</u> name is Patricia.

C

1. who   3. daughter
2. that   4. her

D

<u>Who</u> is <u>that</u>?
That is my <u>daughter</u>.
What is <u>her</u> name?
Her name is Patricia.

Lesson 5 page 58

B

2. b   5. b
3. b   6. g
4. g

C

2. goodbye   5. gas
3. birthday   6. book
4. girl

D

Ⓑrown, Ⓖoes, Ⓑoston, Ⓖalina

E

Answers will vary.

Review and expand page 59

B

2. cold   5. gold
3. sold   6. bold
4. hold

C

2. <u>s</u>old   5. <u>h</u>old
3. <u>b</u>old   6. <u>c</u>old
4. <u>g</u>old

D

Answers will vary.

Unit 7 Do we need apples?

Lesson 1 page 60

A

2. fruit   6. van
3. four   7. vegetables
4. fifty   8. vent
5. verbs

C

2. <u>first</u> name   6. <u>v</u>an
3. <u>four</u>   7. <u>v</u>ent
4. <u>fifty</u>   8. <u>v</u>erbs
5. <u>v</u>egetables

D

Answers will vary.

Lesson 2 page 61

B

2. no   6. no
3. no   7. yes
4. yes   8. no
5. yes

C

I like cheese.
My husband likes beef.
My daughter likes chicken.
We all like rice.

D

I like <u>cheese</u>⊙
My husband likes <u>beef</u>⊙
My daughter likes <u>chicken</u>⊙
We all like <u>rice</u>⊙

Lesson 3 page 62

A

2. He doesn't like chicken.
3. They like fruit.
4. He doesn't need rice.
5. She needs chicken.

B

She likes chicken.
He doesn't like chicken.
They like fruit.
He doesn't need rice.
She needs chicken.

C

Answers will vary.

Lesson 4 page 63

B

Flor: Can you help <u>me</u>?
Clerk: Yes.
Flor: I <u>need</u> apples.
Clerk: <u>Here</u> you <u>go</u>.

C

1. me   3. here
2. need   4. go

D

```
M A E L H Ⓝ I
B Ⓗ E R E Ⓔ K
V I T Q R Ⓔ J
X M U N Z Ⓓ Ⓜ
C S L Ⓖ Ⓞ G Ⓔ
N E E B R V O
```

Lesson 5 page 64

B

2. middle   5. beginning
3. end   6. end
4. beginning

C

2. beginning   5. end
3. beginning   6. middle
4. end

D

Ⓕruit, Ⓥegetable, coⓕfee, beeⓕ

E

Answers will vary.

Review and expand page 65

B
2. r<u>i</u>ce   5. m<u>i</u>ce
3. pr<u>i</u>ce   6. d<u>i</u>ce
4. sl<u>i</u>ce

C
2. r<u>i</u>ce   5. <u>s</u>lice
3. <u>d</u>ice   6. price
4. <u>m</u>ice

D
Answers will vary.

Unit 8 Take Two Tablets

Lesson 1 page 66

A
2. hand   6. sick
3. head   7. shoes
4. husband   8. shirt
5. son

C
2. <u>h</u>ead   6. <u>s</u>on
3. <u>h</u>usband   7. <u>sh</u>irt
4. <u>H</u>ana   8. <u>sh</u>oes
5. <u>s</u>ick

D
Answers will vary.

Lesson 2 page 67

B
2. no   6. yes
3. yes   7. no
4. no   8. yes
5. yes

C
My family is sick.
My daughter has a cold.
My son has an earache.
My husband has a sore throat.
I have a headache.

D
My family is <u>sick</u>⊙
My daughter has a <u>cold</u>⊙
My son has an <u>earache</u>⊙
My husband has a <u>sore throat</u>⊙
I have a <u>headache</u>⊙

Lesson 3 page 68

A
2. He has a sore throat.
3. They have the flu.
4. They have a cough.
5. He has a headache.

B
She has a stomachache.
He has a sore throat.
They have the flu.
They have a cough.
He has a headache.

C
Answers will vary.

Lesson 4 page 69

B
Receptionist: <u>Hello</u>. Downtown Clinic.
Hana: <u>This</u> is Hana Smith. I need to see the doctor.
Receptionist: <u>What</u> is the matter?
Hana: I have a <u>stomachache</u>.

C
1. hello   3. what
2. this   4. stomachache

D
1. Hello   3. What
2. This   4. stomachache

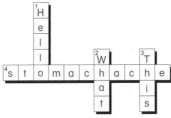

Lesson 5 page 70

B
2. <u>s</u>   5. <u>s</u>
3. <u>sh</u>   6. <u>h</u>
4. <u>sh</u>

C
2. sick   5. she
3. shoes   6. headache
4. six

D
Sh⊙pper'⊙, table⊙poon⊙, ⊙ix, hour⊙.

E
Answers will vary.

Review and expand page 71

B
2. <u>gr</u>eet   5. b<u>ee</u>t
3. <u>str</u>eet   6. <u>sh</u>eet
4. <u>f</u>eet

C
2. <u>f</u>eet   5. <u>sh</u>eet
3. <u>gr</u>eet   6. <u>str</u>eet
4. <u>b</u>eet

D
Answers will vary.

Unit 9 What size?

Lesson 1 page 72

A
2. year   6. who
3. winter   7. white
4. wife   8. where
5. when

C
2. yellow   6. when
3. winter   7. where
4. wife   8. who
5. white

D
Answers will vary.

Lesson 2 page 73

B
2. no   6. no
3. yes   7. yes
4. no   8. no
5. yes

C
It's July.
I'm wearing white shorts.
I'm wearing a red T-shirt.
I'm wearing a blue cap.

D
It's July⊙
I'm wearing <u>white</u> shorts⊙
I'm wearing a <u>red</u> T-shirt⊙
I'm wearing a <u>blue</u> cap⊙

Lesson 3 page 74

A
2. She is wearing a skirt.
3. She is wearing black shoes.
4. They are wearing white coats.
5. She is wearing a white coat and shoes.

B
He is wearing a shirt.
She is wearing a skirt.
She is wearing black shoes.
They are wearing white coats.
She is wearing a white coat and shoes.

C
Answers will vary.

Lesson 4 page 75

B
Yen: I'm <u>looking for</u> a T-shirt.
Clerk: What <u>size</u>?
Yen: <u>Small</u>.

C
1. looking   3. size
2. for   4. small

D
1. looking   3. size
2. for   4. Small

Lesson 5 page 76

B
2. <u>y</u>   5. <u>wh</u>
3. <u>w</u>   6. <u>y</u>
4. <u>wh</u>

C
2. where   5. yellow
3. wife   6. who
4. when

D

$\widehat{W}$hat's, $\widehat{W}$eekend, $\widehat{W}$eather, $\widehat{W}$arm, $\widehat{W}$indy.

Review and expand page 77

B

2. due
3. Sue
4. glue

C

2. Sue
3. glue
4. due

D

Answers will vary.

Unit 10 Where's the bank?

Lesson 1 page 78

A

2. lamp   6. park
3. laundromat   7. post office
4. library   8. pencil
5. paper

C

2. library   6. park
3. lamp   7. pencil
4. list   8. paper
5. post office

D

Answers will vary.

Lesson 2 page 79

B

2. no   6. yes
3. no   7. yes
4. yes   8. no
5. no

C

My apartment building is on
Pine Street.
There's a restaurant next to the
laundromat.
There's a park on the corner.
I go to the park on Saturdays.

D

My apartment building is on Pine
Street⊙
There's a restaurant next to the
laundromat⊙
There's a park on the corner⊙
I go to the park on Saturdays⊙

Lesson 3 page 80

A

2. There are two lamps.
3. There is a list.
4. There are two pencils.
5. There is a park.

B

There is a library.
There are two lamps.
There is a list.
There are two pencils.
There is a park.

C

Answers will vary.

Lesson 4 page 81

B

Lila: Excuse me. Where is the
      library?
Paul: It's next to the park.
Lila: Thank you.
Paul: You're welcome.

C

1. where   3. you
2. next   4. welcome

D

1. Where   3. you
2. next   4. welcome

	¹W					³y		²n
	h							
⁴w	e	l	c	o	m	e		e
	r					u		x
	e							t

Lesson 5 page 82

B

2. beginning   5. beginning
3. end   6. end
4. middle

C

2. beginning   5. middle
3. middle   6. end
4. beginning

D

$\widehat{p}$olice, hospita$\widehat{l}$, $\widehat{p}$ost office

E

Answers will vary.

Review and expand page 83

B

2. pot   5. hot
3. cot   6. not
4. tot

C

2. not   5. hot
3. cot   6. tot
4. pot

D

Answers will vary.

Unit 11 This Is My Home

Lesson 1 page 84

A

2. kit   6. read
3. Kara   7. ruler
4. room
5. refrigerator

C

2. kindergarten 5. refrigerator
3. Kara   6. ruler
4. room   7. read

Lesson 2 page 85

B

2. yes   6. no
3. no   7. yes
4. no   8. yes
5. yes

C

This is my home.
There is one bedroom and one bath-
room.
There is a red sofa in the living room.
There are two windows above the sofa.
I like my home.

D

This is my home⊙
There is one bedroom and one
bathroom⊙
There is a red sofa in the living room⊙
There are two windows above the sofa⊙
I like my home⊙

Lesson 3 page 86

A

2. Mr. Reza's house is big.
3. Rosa's table is in the kitchen.
4. Joe's TV is in the living room.
5. Kofi's bed is small.

B

Kara's house is small.
Mr. Reza's house is big.
Rosa's table is in the kitchen.
Joe's TV is in the living room.
Kofi's bed is small.

Lesson 4 page 87

B

Kofi: Is there an apartment for rent?
Manager: Yes.
Kofi: How many bedrooms are there?
Manager: Two.

C

2. apartment
3. many
4. two

D

1. there   3. many
2. apartment   4. Two

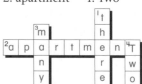

Lesson 5 page 88

B

2. middle   5. end
3. end   6. middle
4. beginning

C

2. middle   5. beginning
3. beginning   6. end
4. middle

D

Apa(r)tment, fo(r) (R)ent, 2B(R), (K)itchen, (R)ent, (K)a(r)en

E

Answers will vary.

Review and expand page 89

B

2. rug   5. mug
3. bug   6. jug
4. hug

C

2. mug   5. jug
3. rug   6. hug
4. bug

D

Answers will vary.

Unit 12 Yes, I Can

Lesson 1 page 90

A

2. jacket   5. zip code
3. June   6. Zita
4. July   7. zero

C

2. July   5. zip code
3. June   6. zero
4. jacket   7. Zita

D

Answers will vary.

Lesson 2 page 91

B

2. yes   6. no
3. no   7. yes
4. no   8. yes
5. yes

C

My brother is a mechanic.
He can fix cars.
My friend is a truck driver.
She can drive trucks.
I want a job.

D

My brother is a mechanic⊙
He can fix cars⊙
My friend is a truck driver⊙
She can drive trucks⊙
I want a job⊙

Lesson 3 page 92

A

2. He can use a computer.
3. He can't fix cars.
4. Can he fix computers? Yes, he can.
5. Can she fix cars? Yes, she can.

B

She can drive a truck.
He can use a computer.
He can't fix cars.
Can he fix computers? Yes, he can.
Can she fix cars? Yes, she can.

C

Answers will vary.

Lesson 4 page 93

B

John: Can you <u>use</u> a <u>computer</u>?
Zita: Yes, I can.
John: Can you <u>work</u> in the <u>evening</u>?
Zita: Yes, I can.

C

1. use   3. work
2. computer   4. evening

D

1. use   3. work
2. computer   4. evening

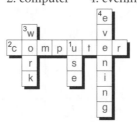

Lesson 5 page 94

B

2. z   5. j
3. z   6. z
4. j

C

2. job   5. jacket
3. July   6. June
4. zero

D

(j)ob, (J)une, (J)uly, (Z)ita

E

Answers will vary.

Review and expand page 95

B

2. <u>B</u>ob   4. <u>r</u>ob
3. <u>c</u>ob   5. <u>s</u>ob

C

2. <u>c</u>ob   4. <u>B</u>ob
3. <u>s</u>ob   5. <u>r</u>ob

D

Answers will vary.

Word Patterns

ab	ag	an	ack
cab	bag	ban	back
dab	rag	pan	pack
gab	gag	can	hack
jab	sag	ran	quack
tab	hag	Dan	Jack
	tag	tan	rack
	lag	fan	lack
	wag	van	sack
	nag	man	Mack
			tack

all	and	ad	am
ball	band	bad	dam
hall	hand	mad	ram
call	land	dad	ham
mall	sand	pad	Sam
fall		fad	jam
tall		sad	yam
gall		had	Pam
wall		lad	

ap	ar	ay	ash
cap	bar	bay	bash
nap	car	may	lash
gap	far	day	cash
rap	jar	pay	mash
lap	mar	gay	dash
sap	tar	ray	rash
map		hay	gash
tap		say	sash
		jay	hash
		way	
		lay	

at	eat	ed	eed
bat	beat	bed	deed
pat	meat	red	need
cat	feat	fed	feed
rat	neat	Ted	reed
fat	heat	led	heed
sat	peat	wed	seed
hat	seat	Ned	
vat			
mat			

ell	en	end	et
bell	Ben	bend	bet
Nell	men	rend	net
cell	den	end	get
sell	pen	send	pet
dell	hen	fend	jet
tell	ten	tend	set
fell	Ken	lend	let
well	yen	vend	wet
hell		mend	met
yell			yet
jell			

ick	id	ig	ill
Dick	bid	big	bill
quick	did	jig	kill
kick	hid	dig	dill
Rick	kid	pig	mill
lick	lid	fig	fill
sick		rig	pill
Nick		gig	gill
tick		wig	quill
pick			hill
wick			sill
			ill
			till
			Jill
			will

im	in	ip	it
dim	bin	dip	bit
Tim	din	rip	pit
him	pin	hip	fit
vim	sin	sip	quit
Kim	fin	lip	hit
Jim	tin	tip	sit
rim	gin	nip	kit
	win	zip	wit
	kin	quip	lit

ob	ock	od	og
Bob	dock	cod	bog
lob	hock	pod	jog
cob	lock	God	cog
mob	mock	rod	log
fob	rock	mod	dog
rob	sock	sod	tog
gob		nod	fog
sob			hog
job			

op	ot	ow	ow
bop	cot	bow	bow
sop	not	row	cow
cop	got	know	how
top	pot	sow	now
hop	hot	low	sow
mop	rot	tow	vow
pop	jot		
	tot		
	lot		

ub	uck	uff	ug
cub	buck	buff	bug
pub	muck	cuff	mug
dub	duck	muff	dug
rub	suck	puff	pug
hub	luck		hug
sub	tuck		rug
nub			jug
tub			tug
			lug

un	ut	y	ee
bun	but	by	bee
pun	jut	my	fee
fun	cut		see
run	nut		tee
gun	gut		wee
sun	rut		
nun	hut		

ib	sh	iss	ix
bib	dish	hiss	fix
fib	fish	kiss	mix
rib	wish	miss	six
crib			

o
go
no
so